Chester
CITY OF GHOSTS

T0347463

First published 2021

The History Press
97 St George's Place, Cheltenham,
Gloucestershire, GL50 3QB
www.thehistorypress.co.uk

Text © Mary Ann Cameron, 2021

The right of Mary Ann Cameron to be identified as the Author
of this work has been asserted in accordance with the
Copyright, Designs and Patents Act 1988.

All rights reserved. No part of this book may be reprinted
or reproduced or utilised in any form or by any electronic,
mechanical or other means, now known or hereafter invented,
including photocopying and recording, or in any information
storage or retrieval system, without the permission in writing
from the Publishers.

British Library Cataloguing in Publication Data.
A catalogue record for this book is available from the British Library.

ISBN 978 0 7509 9673 0

Typesetting and origination by Typo•glyphix, Burton-on-Trent
Printed and bound in Great Britain by TJ Books Limited

Chester
CITY OF GHOSTS

Mary Ann Cameron

The
History
Press

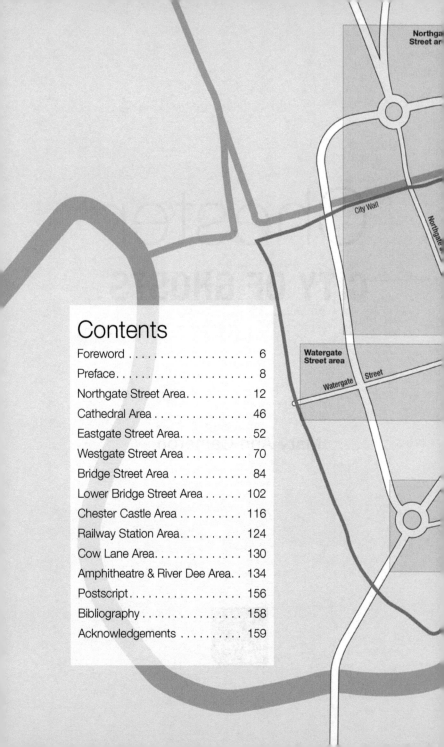

Contents

Northgate
Street area

City Wall

Northgate

Watergate
Street area

Watergate   Street

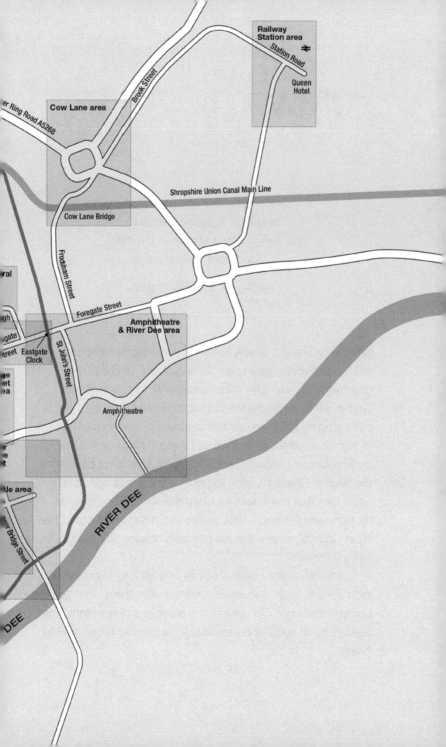

Railway
Station area

Station Road

Queen
Hotel

Cow Lane area

Brook Street

er Ring Road A5268

Shropshire Union Canal Main Line

Cow Lane Bridge

Frodsham Street

Foregate Street

ral

gh

gate

Eastgate
Clock

St John's Street

Amphitheatre
& River Dee area

Amphitheatre

le area

DEE

RIVER DEE

er Bridge Street

Foreword

From ghoulies and ghosties
and long-leggedy beasties
And things that go bump in the night,
Good Lord, deliver us!

(Traditional Scottish Prayer)

Whether you are a deeply religious person or a complete atheistic sceptic, there is something about 'ghoulies and ghosties' that humanity finds fascinating. In a world that seems, sadly, to eschew much of organised religion, there is still a longing for elements that are outside the normal frame of human experience and we call these 'Things of the Spirit'.

The former Cathedral and Collegiate Church of St John the Baptist Chester brings together a quietness and deep spirituality that have even touched the agnostic or atheist; as Mary Ann Cameron later points out, it has been called the 'Thin Church', where the veil between heaven and earth is at its very thinnest.

Certainly, whilst I cannot speak to a ghostly experience in St John's, I can certainly empathise with 'things that go bump in the night', for amidst the quietness of the night I can testify that all sorts of noises make themselves felt as well as heard.

Foreword

This book takes us through what has been called the most haunted city in England, for Chester does have its multitude of stories and experiences, which come together in the city's Ghost Tours.

I commend this book.

David Chesters, OBE
FRSA, FSA (Scot), BA (Hons) DipTh, Rector of Chester

Preface

I qualified as a Chester Tour Guide in 2005 and during the next ten years I amassed many ghost stories about the city. This led, in 2015, to the publication of the first edition of *Chester City of Ghosts*. However, new ghost stories continue to be told and therefore it is now time to publish a second edition, incorporating all the new ghost activity.

Most of the tales in this book concern the city centre, not the suburbs where houses can be easily identified. The following two had to stay in the book, though:

'Let me tell you about the ghost in my flat,' a young man said after he and his girlfriend had been on one of my ghost tours. From the moment they moved into their flat in a converted old house in a suburb of Chester, they regularly saw a head moving around at floor level. They told nobody, fearing ridicule, until their first Christmas there, when the residents of all the flats in the house came together for a party. Once they were full of Christmas cheer, they told their neighbours the story of the head. There was a stunned silence. Then the people from the flat below them said, 'We've got the body!'

Once people know I am a ghost tour guide, I am often told personal stories. One Christmas I was in a pub in the centre of town, when a lady started chatting to me. When I told her I was a tour guide, she casually remarked: 'Oh, there's a ghost in our house.' She shares her house, she said, with the ghost of an old man. He regularly turned the lights on and off in the breakfast room: it was his favourite room when he was alive and lived there.

People have lived and died in Chester for more than two thousand years during its rich and varied history. They have died peacefully in their beds, accidentally, or violently as a result of a fight or attack. And Chester has certainly been attacked throughout the centuries. First came the Romans, then the Angles and Saxons, the Vikings, William I and the Normans, the Welsh and, finally, Cromwell with his Roundheads. At one point, in the early 900s, Chester was attacked at the same time by Danish, Norwegian and Welsh armies. You will be pleased to know the good people of Chester won that battle, but only thanks to their bees: as a last resort, they threw their beehives over the walls onto the attackers, who promptly fled.

The earliest evidence that has been found of people living on this site is that of Iron Age families, but there is nothing to show who they were or how they lived, although they probably belonged to the local tribe, the Cornovii.

Whoever was there in the second half of the AD 70s, though, soon disappeared when 6,000 Romans, members of the 2nd Legion Adiutrix, arrived and built the first fortress. It was constructed in the usual Roman fortress style of a rectangle with rounded corners, made with a turf and earth rampart and topped by a wooden palisade. This was replaced by the 20th Legion, Legio XX Valeria Victrix, who arrived in AD 90 and stayed until 410. These soldiers built the biggest fortress in the country, 60 acres instead of the normal 50, and the biggest amphitheatre, both of solid, strong, red sandstone. The basic street pattern of this Fortress Deva, named after the Celtic name for the River Dee, is the basic street pattern of the City of Chester today. As you walk along the four main streets, you are walking where Roman soldiers marched centuries ago.

They chose a good site: Chester gives easy access to Wales and the west, and was a good marching distance to other fortresses, such as the present city of York. The Fortress Deva was built at the mouth of the River Dee, which is tidal up to and beyond Chester, so ships from Italy and elsewhere could easily reach the fortress's port along the then very wide estuary.

There were two main changes to the appearance of Chester after the Romans left. The river silted up over the centuries and moved from the base of the Wall in the present-day Nuns Road to its current position at the far side of the racecourse. And at the beginning of the tenth century, Chester's walls were extended down to the river, wrapping around and offering protection to the houses that had been established outside the fortress walls.

In 1070, William Duke of Normandy, William the Conqueror, William I of England arrived in Chester and built a castle, a symbol of dominance and a centre of power in the region for two hundred years. There followed a period of growth, trade and stability in Chester, until the Civil War fighting damaged or destroyed nearly every building within the walls. It did lead to some superb rebuilding in the Georgian era and style, though. And from then on Chester grew as a place to visit, shop, eat and hunt for ghosts.

A question I am often asked is: What do ghosts look like? They make their presence felt in a number of ways. Some, known by the German word *poltergeist*, move things around; others make noises, create an icy atmosphere or a leave a smell. Some appear as though they are a living, breathing person until they do something that startles, such as walk through a wall. I have worked with a colleague whose husband regularly saw ghosts. He was once in a hotel with an open fire. He was sitting by it, reading, when a lady came to put more logs on the fire. It took a while for him to realise that she could not actually pick up the logs, as her hands kept passing through them. On another occasion, my colleague's husband was in a hotel room, preparing for a meeting, when he saw a monk walk through one wall, cross the room, and walk through the wall opposite. The next day he asked the receptionist about the history of the hotel. She just looked at him and said, 'You've seen the monk, haven't you?' Apparently the hotel was built on the site of a monastery, destroyed after the Dissolution of the Monasteries in the sixteenth century.

I am also asked if I have ever seen a ghost. My honest answer is that I do not know whether I have or not. Perhaps I have and simply did not realise. I have been told I can accurately detect their presence, though. I was once in a house in North Wales that the owner told me was haunted. As I moved around the rooms, I successfully detected which rooms were haunted and which were not. On my second visit, I told the owner that I had felt someone walk past me. 'Yes,' came the reply. 'It was the ghost of the housekeeper. Didn't you see her?'

What is special about Chester is the number of new and current sightings of ghost activity. As this book will show, Chester can easily claim to be the most actively haunted town in the country. Indeed, a Celtic Christian has described St John the Baptist's Church in Chester, one of the final stops in this book, as 'a thin church, where the veil between Heaven and Earth is at its thinnest; a deeply Spiritual place'. Whether you believe in ghosts or not, this book and its journey through the streets of the city centre will make you wonder and question. And possibly look over your shoulder. As Samuel Johnson said, 'all argument is against it; but all belief is for it'. Or, as Shakespeare wrote:

'There are more things in heaven and earth, Horatio, than are dreamt of in your philosophy'.

Northgate Street Area

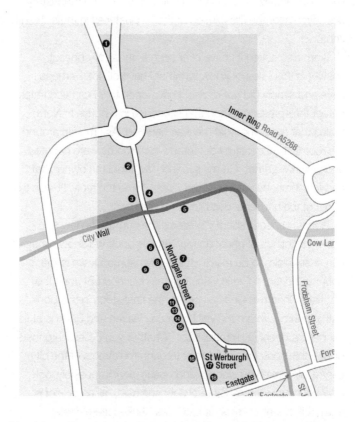

Northgate Street leads from its junction with Eastgate Street, past the Town Hall Square, up to the Northgate and on towards the Wirral, the peninsula between the River Dee and the Mersey estuary. The road and the gate both follow the original Roman routes: Northgate Street was the fortress's Via Decumani and the Northgate its Porta Decumani, the word *decumani* indicating that it was the least important of the fortress's gates and streets, away from the main, prestigious entrance. Nonetheless, it was heavily fortified and, being situated on the highest point of the fortress, gave a good view of the surrounding area.

What you see now is not Roman, though: there is a beautifully graceful arch crossing Northgate Street and linking the left and right sides of the walls. It was designed in 1810 by Thomas Harrison, an architect who was very busy in Chester in the nineteenth century for over forty years. He designed the law courts at Chester Castle, the Commercial News Room off Northgate Street, and the Grosvenor Bridge, as well as a number of beautiful houses. If you stand on the Northgate and look west towards the Welsh hills, you will see another of his designs. On top of the tallest hill, Moel Famau, there are the ruins of the Jubilee Tower, built in 1810 to celebrate George III's jubilee. Sadly, a huge storm in 1896 blew it down, but the ruins are still visible from Chester and still attract walkers.

The present red sandstone gate replaced the medieval gate, a huge construction that included high towers, a portcullis, a gaol, dungeons carved into the rock, and a very narrow gate through which traffic struggled to pass. Until the nineteenth century this was fit for purpose: it was the least important entrance and it provided a suitably forbidding sight for locals, a place of incarceration and execution. It was therefore the last of the gates to be replaced, but by the time of its demolition in 1808, traffic through it had increased with the building of overspill housing to the north of the city. And the authorities had been shamed by a damning report describing the conditions in the gaol. It needed to go. But look over the parapet on the Northgate, down to the pavement below – underneath, the dark, airless dungeons still remain.

Until recently, the city wall to the left of the Northgate was completely hidden from sight and the elements by huge sheets of plastic. In 2011 it was discovered that a flight of steps leading up to the walls, built during the Georgian era, had started to move. Scaffolding was erected to support them and to allow engineers to measure their movement. It was not the first time the steps had moved: in the nineteenth century, it seems, the gap between the inner wall and the steps had simply been filled in. In 2011, to the authorities' horror, though, the engineers discovered that the flight of steps was not actually tied to the inner wall – for the simple reason that the Georgian builders had actually removed the inner wall along the whole of that stretch. Cue a mad rush to erect a network of scaffolding to tie the whole remaining structure to the outer wall, close off the steps, and call in the archaeologists.

Within the walls of Chester, archaeologists must be allowed to examine whenever the ground is disturbed. What they found at this site was truly amazing: the huge sandstone base of the West Tower of the fortress, built by the Legio XX Valeria Victrix, the 20th Legion, about the end of the first century. Even some of the original mortar was visible. What was even more astounding was the discovery of the mud bank erected by the first Romans to set up camp, the Legio II Adiutrix, the 2nd Legion. In the AD 70s, when the 2nd Legion arrived, they quickly established a secure military base with a turf and earth rampart, topped by a timber palisade. The timber has gone, but the rampart is still clearly visible here. These wonderful findings triggered years of checking, planning, designing, careful rebuilding and negotiations with archaeologists, engineers, builders, planners, historians, designers and people holding the purse strings. Work finished in 2020, the walls made safe and secure and have now been reopened. And, of course, the steps have been reinstated for pedestrians – this time securely fixed to an inner wall.

Before you leave the top of the Northgate, look to your left. Along the stretch of the walls leading westwards are Morgan's Mount, Pembertons Parlour and, at the corner where the walls turn to head south, the Water Tower. Old stories relate how Royalist soldiers from the Civil War still man their cannon at Morgan's Mount; genteel ladies take the air at Pemberton's Parlour. And Roundheads at the Water Tower can sometimes still be heard celebrating their victorious siege of the city in 1646.

❶ George and Dragon

But it is time to begin your exploration of Chester's ghosts, starting with a reassuring word. The George and Dragon is a pub and hotel, clearly visible from the Northgate on the other

side of Fountains Roundabout. It is a half-timbered building, erected in the late Victorian era: the inside has been modernised more than once over the years but the outside

remains a mock-Tudor extravaganza. It was built over one of the sites where Roman soldiers were buried, as no burials were allowed within the fortress walls. Stories abound of Roman soldier ghosts walking through the bedrooms, a sentry ghost guarding the honoured dead. But not in this book.

When a Chester tour guide, one of the group who started the original Chester ghost tours a good few decades ago, learnt in 2015 that I was writing the first edition of *Chester City of Ghosts*, she was quick to inform me that she and the other ghost guides had invented that story. It was promptly removed from the book. All the ghost stories in this book, I can assure you, are researched and genuine. But who knows, perhaps recent sightings are also genuine ...

2 11 Upper Northgate Street

This building nestles next to what was obviously a coaching inn before the arrival of the railways. Coaches could draw in under the shelter of the overhanging first-floor bedrooms, so the ladies and gentlemen passengers could alight without getting wet. Both it and 11 Northgate Street were built in the mid-eighteenth century, but it is only number 11 that has a history of ghostly activity. It now houses the Bombay Palace, a very highly rated Asian restaurant.

In December 2013, the owner of the Bombay Palace was alone in the restaurant at 3 a.m. when he heard a noise, a door banging, in the gentlemen's lavatory. He knew the waiter was upstairs in the flat and his family had all gone home, so, fearing a burglar and wanting evidence in case of a future prosecution, he went into the room and took a photo before turning the light on. When he did turn the light on, he could see nobody there. However, when he looked at the photo he had taken, a man's face could clearly be seen in the mirror on the lavatory wall. Customers, a workman and staff had long discussed a feeling of a presence at the back of the restaurant, and an empty coffin had been found in the cellar in the 1980s – whether there is any connection with the man in the lavatory we will probably never know.

3 Blue Coat School

On the same side of the street, near the Northgate, is the Blue Coat School, Chester's first charity school, established to educate boys from poor families. It was built in 1717 and replaced the Little St John's Hospital, founded in 1190 by Earl Ranulph of Chester, with the aim of providing accommodation for '13 poor and feeble men' and with the impressive full title of St John the Baptist without the Northgate and the Hospital of John the Baptist. The building should have crumbled under the weight of that lengthy name but it was only demolished in 1644, just before the Siege of Chester during the Civil War, with the aim of stopping the Roundheads from using it as a base to attack the city.

Above the central entrance arch is a statue of one of the pupils wearing the uniform of the school, with its distinctive blue coat. The school closed in 1949, and by the beginning of this century it was occupied by the History and Archaeology Department of the University of Chester. When the school had been enlarged in the mid-1850s, almshouses were built in a lovely quadrangle behind it, to replace those at the previous hospital. Entrance for the residents was, and is still, under the central arch, which is also the site of the entrances to both wings of the Blue Coat School.

Another entrance to the school was built in 1793, though, but only for those prisoners emerging from the dungeons of the Northgate gaol on the day of their execution. They were allowed to make a short, sad journey along Northgate Street to the school's Chapel of St John the Baptist, to say their last prayers before they were hanged. Too many of them were rescued by friends, however, as they made their way along the street to the chapel, so a slim sandstone bridge was built from the prison directly into the side of the chapel.

This bridge, originally with high, cast-iron railings to prevent escape attempts, became known as the Bridge of Sighs.

While the University of Chester occupied the building, the chapel was used as administrative offices, and when I was at a meeting there once, I insisted on visiting the offices – after all, I was a ghost guide so I was bound to be able to sense a ghostly atmosphere in the room where all those distraught prisoners had said their last goodbyes. But there was nothing and so, noting my disappointment, the lecturer who was showing me round offered to show me the headmaster's study, then being used as a seminar room. It was a beautiful oak-panelled room but in one corner there was a wooden box about five feet high, divided in two, each half with a square cut out at face level, the holes filled with spaced vertical wooden rods. 'What is that?' I asked. It was, I was told, where the headmaster put the naughty boys.

As I heard the answer, I immediately felt my shoulders, then my scalp, begin to itch unbearably, while the lecturer watched my hair begin to stand on end. When the itching became intolerable, I simply had to leave the room, only to meet another lecturer who sympathised with me. When she had been allocated that room for seminars, she stayed in there only a few seconds before leaving and refusing to teach there because of the oppressive atmosphere.

As I told this story, other staff began to tell me their own tales. The building's basement has no opening windows or doors to the outside, and therefore no possibility of draughts. Yet a thick wooden door would often slam shut, even though it was too heavy to move easily.

One of the university cleaners hated working there: one evening while she was cleaning on the first floor, she heard her boss shouting her name urgently, so she dropped everything and ran towards her, only to bump into her boss running to find her because she had heard the cleaner crying her name.

The university left the Blue Coat School in 2010 and since then it has been renovated and now houses the Bluecoat Centre for Charities and Voluntary Organisations. During the renovations another two skeletons were uncovered and reburied. Later, after the opening, I and other tour guides were invited to look round the building and admire the newly furbished interior. We were greeted in the headmaster's study and I was very relieved to discover that all the negative atmosphere had disappeared, as had the wooden box.

4 2—4 Upper Northgate Street

Directly opposite the Blue Coat School is an elegant pair of Georgian houses, built in about 1800 and now the home of Northgate Dental Health. The houses are described as having three storeys with basements but little publicity is given to what is in those basements.

Numbers 2 and 4 Upper Northgate Street were built on the site of a seventeenth-century House of Correction, and in one basement there is a hole in the lower part of a wall leading to a small, brick-lined chamber. This is believed to be a cell in the House of Correction, possibly the Little Ease, a room where a solitary prisoner could neither sit, stand or lie. When they emerged, they had often lost the ability to walk. One story of the Little Ease tells of a rather corpulent man who was imprisoned there for the dreadful crime of being a Quaker. The gaolers found it difficult to get him into the cell because of his size. And in the morning they found him dead of suffocation. Whether it is the Little Ease or not, ghosts are still trapped down there. Staff who arrive early in the morning can often clearly hear men talking in the cellar near this hole. Some have even seen a man walking round in the cellar.

But in the last few years, the ghosts have taken to wandering around the building. In September 2016, a receptionist went up the steps to the front door to open up the surgery. As she did so, she could clearly hear laughter in the adjoining reception area. As she put her hand and the key towards the lock, something pushed her hand to the door. When she unlocked the door and opened it, the laughter stopped and she walked into an empty reception area.

In November of the same year, a receptionist and dental assistant were locking up the surgery when they heard someone walking up and down in the waiting room on the floor below. The building, of course, was empty.

One dental nurse is still complaining about being hit over the head by an X-ray tube in a consulting room. The tube is necessarily difficult to move but some invisible force had no problem that day.

5 5 City Walls

At 5 City Walls is Hypha, a vegan restaurant. As you walk from Northgate Dental Health over the canal towards the Northgate, you will see the city walls rising up in front of you. Look for the long ridge of stone about two-thirds of the way up the walls; the section below that ridge is the original Roman section. The height has been raised over the centuries as the city changed from a fortress to a fortified town, to a genteel city, to a major tourist destination. At the same time, shops appeared along some of the length. Hypha is one of these shops, visible behind this section of the walls.

In 2005, when I qualified as a tour guide, number 5 used to be the Mediterranean restaurant and the manager was a student of mine at West Cheshire College (now Cheshire College South and West). When he learnt I was going to do ghost tours, he immediately insisted I included the ghost in his restaurant. I thought he was joking, of course, and laughingly told a student in another group who worked in the restaurant as a waitress. She actually confirmed the story. When she went for an interview for the post of waitress, the manager asked her to go to the kitchen to collect something he needed. A strange thing to ask during an interview, she thought, but of course she went upstairs to the empty kitchen, picked up the item – and immediately felt as though someone behind her was going to attack her. She ran back from the kitchen white-faced with fear, to find all the other staff waiting gleefully to see her reaction: to see if she had felt the presence of the chef who had murdered a previous owner of the restaurant in the kitchen. The manager apparently used this as an initiation test for every new member of staff, to see if they could feel the ghost. The waitress never went in the kitchen alone again.

The new owner, Nick, who acts as both cook in the kitchen and waiter in the restaurant, also lives in the flat above. He has seen, felt and heard nothing since he moved in. The ghost must be very satisfied with the menus.

6 65 Northgate Street

This building, known as the Blue Bell, dates back to the fifteenth century. It is said to be the oldest domestic medieval building in Chester that is still complete. It is therefore Grade I listed, which means it is important enough historically for it to be preserved for posterity – good news for the ghost or ghosts who live there. It was actually two houses originally, which were made into one in the eighteenth century, and is timber-framed with rendered brick covering most of the surfaces. The first-floor rooms jut out, forming a covered archway over the pavement – no one, but no one, walks through the arcade, under the overhanging first floor, without instinctively ducking their heads.

The Blue Bell started life as an inn, being granted its first licence to serve ale in 1494. Since the 1980s, however, it has been a restaurant and is currently El Gato Negro, a tapas bar and grill. Sometimes customers are served in the medieval cellars, if they are brave enough.

Many of the ghost tours make a stop at the Blue Bell because of the sad, romantic ghost who haunts the upstairs room on the left. Her name is Henrietta and she lived there during the Civil War with her family. At that time the city was crowded with Royalist soldiers, who were billeted wherever they could find a welcome. The young Royalist gentleman who stayed in Henrietta's family home fell in love with her, of course, and as he rode off with his fellow soldiers to fight in the Battle of Rowton Heath in September 1645, he promised to marry her on his return. Henrietta sat by the window on the first floor and waited. But he never returned. The Battle of Rowton Heath was a catastrophe for Charles I: so many soldiers died that day that it crushed his hopes of raising an army that could defeat Cromwell and his Roundheads. One of the dead soldiers was Henrietta's lover: Henrietta can sometimes be seen at the upstairs window, still waiting for him to return.

A few years ago I was told a sequel to this story: a fellow guide stopped opposite the Blue Bell and told the story of Henrietta to his group. He, of course, had his back to the building so he could tell the story while the group were given a good view of the building. Later, one of the group went into the restaurant for a meal and congratulated the owner for helping with the ghost tour. What did he mean? You know, he said, when you opened the curtain on the right-hand upstairs window, pretending it was Henrietta. The owner told me she most definitely had not touched the curtain. When I suggested that it could have been a member of staff, she took me upstairs to show me why that would have been impossible: while the left-hand window has no curtain but has a chair next to it, ready for Henrietta after customers have left, the right-hand window has a steep staircase running up the wall beneath. No one could either reach over the stairs and draw the curtain or stand on the stairs and move it.

Staff have had frequent experiences of ghostly activity, though. They have heard the cries of a child: could they possibly be the cries of the servant girl who was raped and killed in the kitchen by Roundhead soldiers after they won the Siege of Chester and came flooding into the city?

I recently met a chef who had worked at the Blue Bell in the early years of this century. When he was working in the kitchen, he would often hear someone calling his name, but no one had. One night he fell asleep in one of the comfy armchairs the owner had situated near the ladies' lavatories. He was woken by a voice calling his name and yelling, 'Lee, Lee, wake up, get out!' 'I did,' he said. 'I was absolutely terrified – and I'm an ex-squaddie!'

One Wednesday evening in April 2014, the cook then working there knew he was the last person in the restaurant – but he felt that he was being followed by someone as he checked all the rooms. He even saw the lights in the yard going on and off, despite the fact they were broken. From that moment, whenever he was alone in the building, he always said goodnight to whoever he left there.

7 2 Abbey Green, Rufus Court

Bollicini's restaurant is in part of Rufus Court, which is a lovely place to while away an evening in Chester, although until a few decades ago it was a very neglected, dilapidated corner of the city. However, in 1991 it was redeveloped into an award-winning area that combined the restored eighteenth- and nineteenth-century houses with new buildings to form an eclectic mixture of shops, cafes, wine bars, businesses and, of course, Bollicini's at number 2, Abbey Green.

Abbey Green is a straight street that runs from the entrance to Rufus Court and then down its right-hand side. Bollicini's has been a successful Italian restaurant there for over fifteen years. Previously, other restaurants came, failed and left: success seemed only to be assured when Bollicini's moved out of the main early nineteenth-century Georgian building into the renovated outbuildings. Perhaps the owners wanted to get away from the ghost on the stairs of the lady in grey. A previous manager of Bollicini's told me none of the staff liked to go up the stairs because they could either see or feel the ghost. Some even saw her with two young children and believed these were the ghosts of the children that the lady, their governess, had murdered. When I told this tale on one ghost tour, one member of the group said she had also felt uncomfortable and uneasy when she had gone up the stairs, but she said the atmosphere in the ladies' lavatory in a first-floor room was so oppressive she had to leave as soon as possible.

Staff have no problem, though, I was told, with the ghost in the cellar. 'What ghost, what cellar?' I asked. I was then taken down to the cellar where the ghost, supposedly a priest, had died when the tunnel, leading from 2 Rufus Court to what is now Chester Cathedral, is believed to have collapsed. The bricked-up entrance to the tunnel was still clearly visible in the cellar. And the priest was a benign presence, watching over the manager as she did her stocktaking every evening.

8 71 Northgate Street

This glorious building, which now houses the popular restaurant Chez Jules, is a fine example of the Vernacular

Revival style, half-timbered with oriel windows, and was designed by a student of our local and prolific Victorian architect, John Douglas. The style is perfect for a city such as Chester, but not really for its original function: it opened in 1911 as Chester's fire station. At the time it had three horse-drawn fire engines, but by the time it closed in the 1960s it had five fire engines, petrol driven by this time, of course. The building has three arched bays: two fire engines fitted in each of the central and right-hand bays, one behind the other, and one was housed in the left-hand bay, where the entrance and administrative offices also were. It would have been a sight to behold to see the fire engines leave the building and turn the sharp corner left or right. However, in 1970 the firemen moved to St Anne's Street. All but one, that is. Jack, a long-retired fireman with fine moustaches, an old-fashioned uniform and a brass helmet, still waits for the bell to ring so he can spring into action.

A few years ago, during a Northgate Street festival, I met a retired fireman who was in charge of a display of old fire engines. I asked him about Jack and he said that yes, late at night he and his colleagues often heard strange noises. But, he added with a smile, it was only the central heating cooling down.

However, in 2017 I was eating lunch with a group from the Wirral and one lady told the story of an incident that had happened at a family meal there a few years earlier. She had been talking to her grandson, who was sitting facing the room, when he suddenly became quiet and stared at something behind her. His eyes then steadily tracked across the room and down the stairs before he turned to his grandmother and asked, 'Why is Fireman Sam here?'

In 2019, the owner of Chez Jules told me that many of the forty or more staff who had worked in the restaurant over the years had seen or heard ghostly activity. He had heard for himself noises of something being bumped and footsteps on the floor above when he knew the restaurant was empty. He has also felt someone standing behind him and each time, when he has turned round, there has never been anyone there.

9 Firemen's Cottages, Firemen's Square

To the left of Chez Jules is an alleyway leading to Firemen's Square, so named because of the row of six cottages immediately

on the left, built in the 1920s to house some of the firemen who worked in the fire station.

In the 1980s a young man lived in one of the Firemen's Cottages. He often used to stay up into the early hours watching television or playing video games. At that time of night Firemen's Square was completely silent, apart from, sometimes, the sound of someone in high heels walking past the young man's cottage. Whenever he looked out of the window, though, there was never anyone there. After a while, the young man left Chester and moved to New Zealand, obviously to get as far away from ghosts as possible. I hope he succeeded.

10 57 Northgate Street

The Pied Bull dates as far back as the mid-twelfth century but there are no signs of the original building. Inside you may see parts of the old timber frame, but a brick exterior was put in place in 1660 and the ground-floor arcade over the pavement and frontage were added early in the eighteenth century. A sign at the front still indicates the distances to London, Bristol, Bath and Ludlow, showing its long history as a coaching inn. In fact, the Pied Bull is considered to have been continuously a pub or inn longer than any other in the city, as there are records of it serving beer or ale since 1571.

In the days when coaches were the only form of public transport, the Pied Bull stretched a long way down King Street, which leads down the hill to its right. Then, of course, outbuildings would have been necessary to stable the horses, shelter the coaches, and provide space for any necessary repairs. The pub has lost a lot of this land but recently extended further down Northgate Street. It is still a hotel, pub and restaurant but now also has its own microbrewery. And three ghosts.

In the cellar is the ghost of John Davies, who I use, on my tours, as an example of a ghost who does not deserve to be actively haunting. In 1609 he went down the steps into the cellar to fill a jug with beer for a customer. In those days there were no electric beer pumps or lighting, so staff had to make frequent journeys down to the beer barrels in the cellar, thus ensuring that over the years the stone steps became worn, and each evening they would be damp from spilt beer. It was down those same steps that John Davies hurried, carrying the jug in one hand and, for some unknown reason, a knife in the other. He tripped, fell down the stairs, the jug broke into pieces, he ended up at the bottom of the stairs, and the knife ended up firmly and deeply embedded in his stomach. He is still complaining bitterly about his bad fortune to people who venture down into the cellar, but to use an informal Yorkshire word, if you are that gormless, you really do not deserve to be a ghost. Staff have in recent years seen a man in the cellar reading a newspaper, so John Davies is obviously not always in a bad mood.

The second ghost is a young lady who wears a long skirt, a long, white, frilled apron, and a hat with a white frill. She is seen moving between bedrooms 7, 8 and 9 on the first floor. Perhaps a chambermaid still catching up on her cleaning duties?

Finally, an elderly man can sometimes be seen enjoying a pint at a table on the ground floor. He is the ghost of a stableman who fell asleep in the stables after one drink too many. Unfortunately, his pipe was still lit and it set the place on fire, burning him to death.

And now a dramatic story about the Pied Bull, which was told to me in September 2020 by a manager of Cote restaurant in Bridge Street. The manager lived in the Pied Bull between the ages of 2 and 7, because his father was the landlord, and he shared his bedroom on the second floor with his baby brother. One night his brother's crying woke him up, so he went over to comfort him. He noticed very thick fog outside in the street, which surprised him as it was late summer. The sound of hoofbeats drew him to the window, and just as he realised there was no fog at all, directly underneath the window a hooded figure appeared. He remembers both man and horse vividly: the horse was like a Shire horse, jet black with bits of grey; the man wore a black hood and cloak tied with thin rope, with an outfit of black cloth underneath. The man reared the horse up towards the boy, turned the horse round, and then both disappeared back into the fog. The next morning, customers of the Pied Bull and his parents all said it must have been the ghost of the stableman who had died in the fire in the stables. And they all said there had certainly been no fog that night.

11 39 Northgate Street

The Coach House, previously known as the Coach and Horses, has a name that indicates that it, too, used to be a coaching inn. There has been an inn on this site since 1664 but the present building only dates to the nineteenth century, even though it merits being Grade II listed.

Current staff have lots of stories of ghostly activity in the building, including strange noises, doors slamming, someone walking across the bottom of the cellar steps – and always the feeling that someone is with them when they are on the cellar steps. But this ghost story dates back to the 1980s when an elderly gentleman booked a room for the night and ordered a pint of beer. He looked so dispirited that the landlady asked him if he was alright. He told her he was fine, but that his wife had died recently. He would have a drink, go for a walk around the city, and then to his room. The next day the landlady's concern deepened when she realised his bed had not been slept in. She contacted the police, who went to the address he had written in the book, a house in Birkenhead on the Wirral. They found the man had indeed lived there, but that had been eight years previously. He had died of a broken heart just a week after his wife's death. The landlady has since retired, taking that guest book when she left, with the gentleman's name and address written in it by his own hand.

12 The Abbey Gate

I am often told stories by people I meet by accident. This strange story concerns the main entrance to the old Abbey of St Werburgh, whose church became Chester Cathedral in 1541. Until its dissolution by Henry VIII, the abbey was one of the most important in the north-west of England and its entrance reflected its status. It was built in the early

fourteenth century in red sandstone, reputedly by Richard the Engineer, who also built Caernarfon Castle. Now it leads to the elegant Georgian Abbey Square. Above the arches there are three rooms, one of which housed George Marsh during his imprisonment and trial for heresy in 1555. He was burnt at the stake that year in Boughton, now a suburb to the east of Chester. His crime was to practise the wrong religion at the wrong time in England's history: he was a staunch Protestant during the reign of the Catholic Mary I. Is he the gentleman who figures in the story I was told in 2016?

That year, roadworks to the south of the city at the junction of the A483 and the A55 caused tremendous traffic problems in the whole area for many months. One day, in despair at being late for a tour, I phoned for a taxi. Once he learnt the reason for my rush, the taxi driver told me the following tale.

In the evening, taxis are allowed to park opposite the Coach House, to the north of the Abbey Gate. One evening, one of the taxi driver's colleagues picked up a passenger dressed in a black cloak who had emerged from the shadows of the gate's arches. He was pleased to hear the passenger wanted to go to the Halkyn Hills: if you look west between the Town Hall and the Coach House, you will see the Halkyn Hills in the distance, over the border in Wales. A long and nicely lucrative journey, the driver thought. When he reached the Halkyn area, the driver asked for the specific address but was told to keep going straight on. He then reached the long, straight, lonely, unlit road that overlooks the Dee estuary as it stretches along the top of the hills. He asked again and was again told to just keep going. Finally, he asked a third time and this time there was no reply. So he stopped the taxi in the pitch darkness, switched on the interior light, and turned round. The taxi was empty. Another colleague had the same experience a few weeks later and since then, said my driver, no one from that taxi company will ever park at that taxi rank. I check frequently. They never do.

Perhaps the cloaked gentleman simply wanted to join his friends. Most of the Halkyn Hills are riddled with old lead mines, some dating back to Roman times. Some were quite shallow, others delved deeper and deeper as demand for lead grew, creating mile upon mile of tunnels. When demand shrank, mines were abandoned, and the last one closed in 1987. Members of a group of cavers are now back in the mines again, with the aim of mapping all the tunnels. Recently, a friend of mine went down with three other cavers to a large central cavern. Two explored one tunnel while my friend and the fourth member of the team tackled two separate tunnels. At an agreed time, they all met in the central cavern for lunch, and one of the pair asked why the other two had come into their tunnel while they were working. Neither of them had. Yet the pair had both heard two men having a conversation near the entrance to their tunnel. Perhaps they had heard the voices of someone on the surface, I innocently suggested when I heard the story. 'We were 600 feet underground,' came the response. The men's voices have been heard on several occasions by different cavers but my friend is not one of them. You may decide whether he should be happy or disappointed.

13 The Town Hall Square

'Do you know there is someone behind you?' asked a woman on a ghost tour led by a fellow guide a few years ago. Nobody else could see the woman dressed in brown, like a Victorian nurse, standing next to the guide in front of the Town Hall.

Another visitor has told me of seeing a man in a cloak standing outside a shop and the ghost of a bear walking around.

14 The Town Hall

Chester's imposing Victorian Town Hall was opened with
great pomp and ceremony in 1869 by the Prince of Wales,
the future Edward VII, and local MP and four-times prime
minister, William Gladstone. It housed the Council Chamber,
the Assembly Room, the Mayor's suite of rooms, the
Magistrates' Court and, in the basement, the police station
and prison cells. The police station has been greatly reduced
in size and importance while the Magistrates' Court was
moved out and into new premises in 1991.

When I attended a function in the Town Hall a couple of
years ago, I was told that if I wanted to hear ghost stories, I
should speak to the Town Hall Keeper. I found him in his little
office near the entrance. He was watching, he said, ghost
activity on the Town Hall's CCTV. I immediately insisted on
joining him and we both watched as balls of miasma, certainly
too big to be dust particles, floated around the television
screen. The CCTV was pointed at the far right-hand corner of
the Assembly Rooms, and for a very good reason. Previously,
the cleaners had complained about a persistent twanging noise
in that area that distracted and greatly irritated them while they
were cleaning the room after a function. They simply could not
work out what was making the noise. The Town Hall Keeper
soon identified the source: along the left-hand wall of the room
are windows covered by thick curtains that are opened and
closed by long cords, the ends of each wound around hooks to
keep them taut. He flicked one of the cords and it made exactly
the same noise the cleaners had heard. But they were adamant
they were the only ones in the room and no one had been near
the curtains while the noise was being made.

The Town Hall Keeper sees ghosts walking the corridors of the building so often it does not bother him anymore. The visitor who was greeted by a lady at the top of the staircase, the boiler man who saw a coachman walking along the corridor, the man who heard his son talking to a man his father could not see – all these and others are somewhat less sanguine about their experiences, though.

One of the Town Hall Keeper's favourite stories is of hearing dogs barking incessantly in the basement a few years ago. Apparently, they were barking where the police dog kennels used to be. He was less happy about the loud banging on the inside of the door leading to the old Magistrates' Court, though. It started so quickly and ferociously just as he was walking past that it made him jump. Of course, when the banging stopped and he opened the door, there was no one there.

15 Visitor Information Centre (VIC)

The residents of and visitors to Chester are very lucky to have a vibrant and very useful Visitor information Centre right in the centre of the city, occupying the left corner of the Town Hall. This is the first place to go on arrival in Chester for information about where to go and how to get there, as well as being a booking centre for tours and attractions such as Chester Zoo. It is also a must visit before a tourist leaves the city or when a Cestrian needs a present for someone: it is a treasure trove of books and gifts.

However, it has dark secrets. Behind the Visitor Information Centre are storerooms that used to be prison cells serving the Victorian Magistrates' Court in the Town Hall above. Lights often go off for no reason in these rooms, plunging the windowless rooms into darkness. This happened when I was there in a meeting in one of them once, and it is, I can assure you, somewhat disconcerting.

Visitor Information Centre employees often complain about the cold temperature in one room, even when it is hot outside or the central heating is on. There could be one reason: in April 1966 this was the cell where Myra Hindley, the notorious child killer, was held overnight before she was committed to trial at Chester Assizes. Has her evil spirit remained in the cell where she slept?

Some people have seen a lady wearing a brown dress walking across the Centre's floor after closing time. This led to a complaint by one previous member of staff: he had worked there for many years and had never seen a ghost. He was even more irked when a new manager took up the post and immediately started seeing one. Once the VIC had closed for the day and she was working in her office, she would sometimes see images on the CCTV of someone walking across the shop floor. Recently there has been no ghost activity in the VIC. But perhaps they are just waiting for the right person to visit.

16 19 Northgate Street

The White Company at 19 Northgate Street is housed in a row of black and white buildings between the Town Hall Square and St Peter's Church, which is on the corner of Northgate Street and Eastgate Street. They were built between 1897 and 1909, so spanning two centuries and the reigns of two monarchs. John Douglas designed two-thirds of them and James Strong, his pupil, a good number of the others, so it is not surprising they are full of glorious twiddles and twirls. There are also a number of brightly painted statues decorating the first-floor exteriors: a rather splendid one of the then new king, Edward VII, watches over the pedestrians in the Town Hall Square from his perch above the last shop on the row.

Sadly, this rebuild meant the removal of one of the medieval Rows, Shoemakers' Row, but it had disintegrated into an irretrievable state and it did allow the street to be widened, which was sorely needed.

The White Company is the only shop in this row so far, to my knowledge, to have experienced ghost activity. I heard about the first story as I was researching the first edition of this book. In February 2015, the manager was alone in the bedding and linen department upstairs when she heard a thud and found a packaged pillowcase on the floor – but the clear plastic retainer holding it on the shelf had not moved an inch.

A few years later, as I was shopping there, I heard the story of the delivery fairy. This is what the staff call the people who make deliveries to the shop late at night or early in the morning so that everything is ready when the shop opens, without the delivery blocking the street or hindering customers during the day. The staff rarely see the delivery fairy, but one day he was late and the manager was early so they were able to greet each other. The man had one burning question: how do the staff and customers put up with the people in the flat above, on the second floor? The manager asked what he meant. He replied that whenever he did a delivery, whether late at night or early in the morning, he could hear loud noises from the flat above of people stamping around and dragging furniture or something across the floor. It continued the whole time he was delivering. Surely, he thought, the manager could get the landlord to sort them out. There was just one problem with that solution: no one lived on the second floor and the rooms were empty.

17 **22–24 Northgate Street**

The building that currently houses Mountain Warehouse became an electricity showroom in 1924, and its rare

inter-war facade still proudly states it was designed for Chester City Council. It is more coy about advertising its ghost, though.

One day, a few years ago, a young shop assistant who had been working alone on the first floor came downstairs and told the manager she was relieved it was the end of her shift and she could go home. The loud banging had unnerved her and she was unconvinced when the manager told her it was probably just the old woodwork moving. No, it was much louder than that, she said. When she had gone, the manager went upstairs to check and videoed the result on his phone, which is how I was able to see and hear what happened next. The first-floor showroom was completely empty, so at first the video moved slowly around the silent room. Suddenly, without warning, there was a series of very loud bangs, as though someone was using a sledgehammer with great force. The video jerked and the shocked manager expressed his feelings in such a way as to render the video unsuitable for the general public. Nothing has happened since. So far. But in 2017 I was contacted by someone who had worked in the showroom twenty years previously and had heard this story.

She confirmed that staff then were also very wary of the first floor because of the frequent unexplained noises and the constant creepy atmosphere up there.

18 6 Northgate Street

The Scented Garden moved into 6 Northgate Street, on the last remaining Row in this area of the city, in 2015. It offers a range of alternative therapies in a beautifully calm atmosphere and is right above Hotel Chocolat at street level. To me, that sounds like the perfect combination. The first thing the staff did before they opened for business was to cleanse the whole building to remove any negative energy. They had had so many examples of ghost activity in their previous venues that they wanted to ensure the ghosts did not follow them again.

Previously, The Scented Garden was at 7 Bridge Street Row East, where staff experienced a lot of ghostly activity, some quite unsettling. Doors closed on their own, things fell over and lights were constantly going off and on. There were often noises, especially first thing in the morning and last thing at night, when someone could be heard coming down the stairs and jumping off the bottom steps. All the staff were uneasy when on the upstairs corridor and often felt someone leaning over the stairs, watching them. One customer felt very oppressed in the treatment room on that floor. There

were also smells that came and went very quickly. One morning was particularly scary for the manager, when a catalogue of things happened, including poltergeist activity untidying one of the treatment rooms. The final straw was when all the crockery on the drainer in the kitchen was swept onto the floor with a tremendous crash.

Prior to its residence in Bridge Street Row East, The Scented Garden was at the corner of Godstall Lane and Eastgate Row North, where they also experienced a lot of activity – but in this case they were not scared. Staff felt the presence of someone motherly checking they were alright and there were often lovely smells of delicious stews.

Behind every man now alive stand thirty ghosts,
for that is the ratio by which the dead outnumber
the living.

Arthur C. Clarke,
2001: A Space Odyssey

Cathedral Area

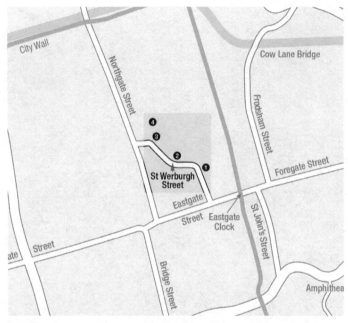

This area of Chester is one of my favourites, with a stunning display of architecture spanning the centuries. The street is named after St Werburgh, the seventh-century daughter of a Mercian king, who became a nun. She ensured her elevation to sainthood after bringing back to life a goose that had been killed by a servant. Its resurrection was truly a miracle because the servant had not only killed the goose, he had roasted and eaten it so thoroughly that only the carcass remained. Although St Werburgh never visited Chester while alive, her bones were brought to Chester in about the year 900 in order to keep them out of the hands of the Danes, who were marauding areas south of Chester. Her relics proved very useful:

when Chester was attacked later, her bones headed a parade of monks and citizens on the walls, and when the monks shook the bones at the enemy, they were blinded and ran away in terror.

St Werburgh Street is dominated by the Cathedral Church of Christ and the Blessed Mary, which started life as the church of the Benedictine Abbey, built by Hugh Lupus, the first Earl of Chester. The first stones were laid in 1092 and building and rebuilding continued until 1537, when there seemed no point, as by then Henry VIII was busy dissolving all the monasteries in England. Henry made the abbey church into a cathedral for his new Church of England, but as the centuries passed, the cathedral fell into very poor repair, both inside and out, and restoration was undertaken by the architect George Gilbert Scott in the mid-nineteenth century. What you actually see, then, when you look at the cathedral, is a skin of Victorian sandstone that covers and protects the original softened red sandstone beneath.

Opposite the cathedral is the oldest building on St Werburgh Street, currently housing Superdrug. The building started life as a chapel in 1348 and since then has been an assembly hall, a court, warehouse, wool market, theatre, music hall, cinema and, finally, a shop.

To the right of the chapel is St Werburgh's Row, built in 1935, and to its left is St Werburgh's Mount, built in the 1870s by John Douglas. The street then bends to the right, leading from the south side of the cathedral in a straight line to Eastgate Street. This section used to be just a narrow alley, but John Douglas doubled the width so shoppers could walk in comfort to the shops he built on the east side in the last decade of the nineteenth century. He finished the row of shops just two years before the death of Queen Victoria with the most outrageous piece of flattery I have ever seen: in a niche above one of the shops is a statue of Victoria, at least five stone lighter than she was in real life.

St Werburgh Street is both an architectural and shopping delight. But it continues to reveal its dark secrets.

1 St Werburgh Street

A few years ago a Chester hairdresser told me of the ghost in the hairdresser's based in the last shop in the row on the east side of St Werburgh Street. When he worked there, the ghost was in the cellar of the building. He and his colleagues believed there was a blocked up tunnel between the cellar and the cathedral. When I heard this story, I immediately went to investigate. The salon had changed hands to the current owners, Supercut, and staff were astonished to hear me talking about the ghost, as they had told nobody since they moved in about the ghost activity they had experienced. It seems the ghost has now moved to the top floor and likes to frighten staff by opening and closing doors that are so stiff the staff themselves have great difficulty opening them.

2 St Werburgh Street

Late at night, trails of miasma are said to float along St Werburgh Street, near Godstall Lane. These are the sad souls of Roundhead and Royalist soldiers who died there in 1645. Charles I had just lost the Battle of Rowton Heath, and the Roundheads managed

to break through the Eastgate, sensing another victory. As they charged up St Werburgh Street on horseback, they were met by a troop of Royalists and a fierce battle was fought. The street was so crowded that even when a soldier was killed, he could not fall off his horse and so his soul could not be grounded; his spirit, and those of his fellow soldiers, still seek sanctuary.

 Cathedral

In September 1645, Charles I commanded his soldiers in the Battle of Rowton Heath, a major defeat for the Royalist cause.

The king was cautious enough not to actively take part in the battle: he and his captain initially watched his men ride out of the city towards Rowton Heath from a good vantage point, the Phoenix Tower, on the north-east corner of Chester's walls. This tower, for reasons of history or tourism, was later renamed King Charles' Tower. That day, though, his captain had a brainwave: he suggested Charles would have a better view from the top of the cathedral bell bower. Charles certainly did have a better view – but he also made himself clearly visible to a Roundhead sniper who took careful aim at the king, fired, missed the king, and killed the captain instead. As the captain fell, dying, to the ground below, his last thoughts were that he had nearly caused the death of his sovereign king. He was so ashamed, so mortified, that his soul still wanders below the old bell tower in the grounds of the cathedral.

I stopped outside the cathedral to tell that tale one evening to a group that included a man who said he could see ghosts. In fact, he said, he knew in advance where I was going to stop and tell a ghost story because he could see the ghosts waiting for me at all the different places. The ghost he could see at that moment was a lady who was standing on the pavement in the middle of St Werburgh Row, outside what was then a branch of my bank. I went in there later on business, but of course I asked if they knew of a ghost in the building. They certainly did. It made its presence felt to such an extent in the cellar where the archives were kept that staff would never go down there alone. They were pleased to know it was a woman, though.

In November 2010, a ghost guide had her photo taken by one of her group on the walls at the cathedral bell tower. When the woman checked the photo on her camera, a ball of miasma could be seen floating above the guide's head.

Inside the cathedral is a large monument to the 1st Duke of Westminster. One day, a tourist took a photo of it – only to later discover a ghostly image in the photo of a man dressed in fifteenth-century clothes, standing next to the monument.

4 Abbey Square

Abbey Square originally housed the brew house, bake houses and kitchen of the abbey. However, by the mid-eighteenth century it was full of rough alehouses and dubious people, so the area was rebuilt with the magnificent Georgian rows of houses you can see now. The pond used for giving horses water to drink was filled in and lawned, and all that remains of the old houses are two seventeenth-century sandstone cottages.

The new houses were built for professional people with good reputations who would enhance the standing of the area. Number 3, however, does little to help. From time to time the whole house fills with the smell of Lily of the Valley. And in the days when the kitchen was in the cellar, the huge, heavy iron stove would sometimes be found moved away from the wall with not a scratch on the floor. Nobody has any explanation for either of these events.

The lawn
Is pressed by unseen feet, and ghosts return
Gently at twilight, gently go at dawn,
The sad intangible who grieve and yearn ...

T.S. Eliot,
To Walter de la Mare

Eastgate Street Area

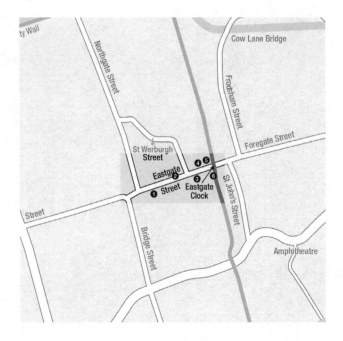

Eastgate Street is full of interesting shops and buildings, it is a place to linger and wander. You could play a game of guess the age of the building as you saunter along, but in this jigsaw of a street you would often be wrong. Eastgate Street stretches from the gate itself westwards to the Cross in the very centre of town. It was the Roman fortress's Via Principalis and the Eastgate was their Porta Principalis Sinistra, its most important entrance. It consisted of two huge semicircular sandstone arches, and through them soldiers would march out on their long journey to York, or their even longer journey to London along what became known as Watling Street.

The Porta Principalis Sinistra was later built over and hidden by a medieval gate of cream sandstone, consisting of two towers with battlements rising four storeys high, above a small arched entrance that was easily closed against enemies. It was probably built in the early fourteenth century, and for many years provided good protection but also warnings to discontented citizens: heads of famous and important miscreants would be placed on pikes above the gate for everyone to see. In 1403 a quarter of the body of Henry Percy, otherwise known as Hotspur (the one who fought Prince Hal and lost, in Shakespeare's *Henry IV Part 1*), was displayed.

My favourite story involving the medieval Eastgate occurred during the Civil War. The Mayor of Chester, Charles Whalley, was woken from his bed one night by the sounds of Roundheads breaking through the outer defences at the far end of Foregate Street. The Mayor just had time to run for his life in his nightshirt up Foregate Street, through the Eastgate, slamming the doors behind him, before the Roundheads started hammering on the doors. As he breathed a sigh of relief, he was dismayed to remember what he had left behind in his house: the mayoral sword and mace. And his wife.

The medieval Eastgate was demolished in 1766 and replaced three years later by the elegant arch that you can see today, the first of the four new gates to be built in Chester over the next few decades. More than a hundred years later, a clock was added. It was made by the famous clockmaker J.B. Joyce of Whitchurch, and John Douglas designed its wonderful wrought-iron plinth. The Eastgate clock is reputed to be the second most photographed clock in the country, although for two years, from 2018 to 2020, it was *the* most photographed clock: Big Ben was covered up for renovation works during that period. The clock was in honour of Queen Victoria's Diamond Jubilee but unfortunately delays meant the opening ceremony took place on her 80th birthday, well over a year later.

The splendid new Eastgate and clock were paid for by the head of the Grosvenor family at the time. The current head of the Grosvenors, the young seventh Duke of Westminster, is one of the richest men in the country, and was the richest person under 30 years of age in the world until he reached that significant birthday in 2021 (he is also very good looking, intelligent and single, but I am sure that is of no interest to you). His main residence is on the outskirts of Chester. The Grosvenor Estate also owns a good number of properties in Chester, including, unsurprisingly, the Grosvenor Hotel. The present hotel was built in the 1860s, about the same time as the gloriously decorated red-brick building opposite. This is another John Douglas masterpiece which started life as the North and South Wales Bank on the ground floor and the Grosvenor Club for gentlemen above. The whole building is now the HSBC bank but signs of its previous lives are still visible: the frieze above the ground-floor windows shows the coats of arms of the twelve former shires of Wales, and above the first-floor windows is the Grosvenor coat of arms. Look for the little dog above the shield. This is a Talbot hunting dog and the first Grosvenor to step foot in England did so with William Duke of Normandy, as his leader of the hunt.

Further along this side of Eastgate Street is another bank, again built in the middle of the nineteenth century. It was the last building in Chester to adopt the classical style and it is, you will note, the only one in this part of the city with no Row running through it. At that time, Eastgate Row North was populated at night by groups of ne'er-do-wells and neither the owners nor the architects wanted them walking along the Row through their bank at night. It meant applying to the City Improvement Committee for permission to close it, and although it had been decided two centuries ago never again to block the Rows, permission was granted. Perhaps the donation of a strip of land that allowed the council to widen St Werburgh Street helped them make their decision?

Every building along Eastgate Street is of historic interest, most Grade II listed, some completely built in one era, others spanning centuries. It is not surprising that a few of them have memories.

❶ 4 Eastgate Row South

4 Eastgate Row South, currently a branch of TSB bank, is overshadowed by its more showy neighbours but nonetheless is Grade II listed. The staff of the TSB bank that now occupies this building are sure there has been no ghostly activity here in the last fifteen years. But as you walk past, look up at the left-hand window on the second floor – sometimes a body can be seen hanging by the neck from a rope. This is the ghostly body of a woman who hanged herself in that room in 1899, after being jilted at the altar.

❷ 9 Eastgate Row North

The Boot is on part of the site of the house where the commander of the Roman Fortress Deva lived. By the early 1660s it was a medieval merchant's house, with wattle-and-daub walls and seventeenth-century oak panelling in the long upstairs room. In 1643, however, it became a pub: the city was crowded with soldiers hanging around waiting for orders during the Civil War and so there was a greatly increased need for places to provide ale.

By the mid-eighteenth century, entry to the pub was down an alley to the rear of the premises, accessed both by patrons of the pub and also those of the brothel it housed upstairs. That alley has now been incorporated into the shop next door. The brothel, I can assure you, has disappeared. But one lady of the night remains, and when I first heard of her, she immediately became my favourite ghost in the whole city. This lady can still be heard in the Boot, late at night, apparently enjoying her work.

The Boot is a wonderful and very popular place for a good drink. And in the back room you can still sit on the wooden settle where ladies would have a drink with their new man friend while they discussed terms and conditions of the evening's activities. At the same time, they would keep an eye on the box, still on the back wall, which indicated when one of the bedrooms had become vacant, so the lady and her gentleman friend could go up and enjoy some privacy. The bedrooms have long gone but the panelled room remains and my favourite ghost is very fond of it. An ex-colleague told me the story of when she worked there as a student. Whenever she left the panelled room, which she was preparing for a private dinner, the poltergeist would move things around, disturbing her table settings time after time. The only way to stop her, my ex-colleague said, was to stand in the middle of the room and shout at her to stop her games.

On the Row level of the pub, a barmaid saw a man in a cape and top hat behind the bar a few years ago. Things get moved, too: one regular customer once saw the lemon tongs slide across the bar by themselves.

And in 2018 I treated a group of actors from Storyhouse's superb Grosvenor Park Open Air Theatre to a ghost tour. We ended up, of course, having a drink in the Boot Inn, and one of the cast took three photos of us all sitting by the front window. As she took them, she felt something walk past her. And when she looked at the photos, there was a large ball of miasma on the left of the first photo, between her and the actors; on the second photo the ball of miasma had moved to the centre; in the third it had moved to the right of the photo. I was thrilled my favourite ghost had come downstairs to join us.

There is also the ghost of a man in the cellar that, to my surprise, is at street level in part of the medieval undercroft behind the shop below. He has not been seen recently but the gas for the beer is turned off from time to time, even though there is nobody down there.

Two years ago I was giving a ghost tour for the lady who lived in a haunted house in Wales. As we approached the Boot, she said could feel the presence of someone called Maria, a friendly presence who wanted to envelop her with kindness. The lady felt nothing when she was inside the pub, but as we left and walked to the Cross, she could still feel Maria pulling her back. Is Maria, I wonder, my favourite ghost from upstairs in the pub, or another Victorian lady of the night?

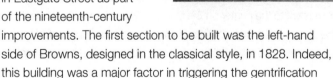

3 4–40 Eastgate Street

Browns of Chester was one of the first shops to appear in Eastgate Street as part of the nineteenth-century improvements. The first section to be built was the left-hand side of Browns, designed in the classical style, in 1828. Indeed, this building was a major factor in triggering the gentrification of Chester: a drawing of the street in 1829, just after it opened, shows a dirty, unpaved street and the Rows festooned with washing lines and drying clothes; a drawing two years later shows a genteel scene of a clean street, tidy Rows empty of flapping linen, and well-dressed ladies walking sedately along the street. Thirty years later, the right-hand extension was built in the Early Gothic style, a nod to the medieval crypt below. Browns became known as the Harrods of the North, and when it was taken over by Debenhams it became the only shop in its portfolio allowed to keep its original name. Sadly, the Debenhams chain of stores was one of the many businesses to succumb to the events of 2020, and on 12 May 2021 Browns of Chester closed its doors after trading in the city for 230 years. But stories about the building linger on.

In the spring of 2021, I had the privilege of meeting Maria Barnard, a Senior Sales Advisor at Debenhams for over nineteen years. Maria loved her job, loved the building, and was very willing to tell me, 'All the ghost stories I can remember.'

Following the extension to the shop in 2001–02, Maria related, homeware was being moved to a new area. One evening, crockery had been stacked on free-standing fixtures either side of the lift, ready to be moved the next day. However, in the morning, every item of crockery was found on the floor, smashed, although the shelving had not moved at all.

In about 2002, a member of the Loss Prevention team noticed knives fell on the floor whenever she walked past the display, a whole set at a time, even though they were firmly fixed to the wall.

Within the last ten years, two members of staff have had to stay in the shop overnight because the alarm system was not working. One of them went to the offices on the second floor to send a document to the printer on the first floor. When he went to collect the document, it was not there; he assumed it had not printed for some reason so returned to the second floor to send it to the printer

again. He then returned to the first floor. This time he found both printed sheets: they had both been screwed into balls and thrown on the floor of the printing room. Other members of staff have seen a lady during office hours around the area where the printer is located; they describe her as wearing a 'large, grand dress'.

The offices on the second floor are actually above what was originally the ballroom. The corridor leading to them is always freezing, whatever the weather, the time of year or the central heating setting.

In one of these offices, nothing would stick to the walls. Whether adhesive tape or drawing pins were used, whatever was fixed to the walls would always later be found on the floor.

A gentleman dressed in a smart suit has been seen walking along this corridor before disappearing into a room. Is this the same gentleman seen in 2017 on the Row outside Browns? During one of my ghost tours, I was told of a young man who was standing on the Row outside Browns when he saw a man, wearing a top hat and suit and carrying a cane, walk towards and then past him. As the man walked, he nodded and greeted everyone he passed. But the young man was the only one who could see him.

Maria told of the little boy who haunted the basement area of the shop for the last few years of trading at Browns, especially in the area next to what was the cafe, where the toy section used to be. He frightened one member of staff by shouting 'Boo!' and one of Maria's colleagues distinctly heard a voice, seemingly coming from one of the toys, saying, 'Play with me.' Another colleague regularly saw the little boy hiding.

At the back of the basement are the loading bays and two paintwork rooms where paint used to be stored. In 2017 or 2018, a child's footprint was found on the floor of one of the loading bays. The footprint was perfectly visible as it was in luminous yellow paint. The source of this paint could only have been the tin in the paint room, which was on a shelf, with its lid firmly sealed. Maria still has a photo of the footprint.

The little boy is not alone in the basement, though. Two members of staff have seen a lady in a long, black dress there. The lady even spoke to one of the members of staff: 'So dusty down here!' One woman assumed it was her friend talking. But her friend was upstairs on the shop floor.

Before I met Maria, I only had three ghost stories concerning Browns. One is related above; the other two are as follows, both also related by members of a ghost tour:

A number of years ago the security officer, having locked up all around the store, could not then manage to activate the burglar alarm. When he went to investigate, he found all the doors had been unlocked. He was alone in the building but someone was playing tricks.

A temporary member of staff was stocktaking when all the hangers in one area of the stockroom started rattling, even though there was nobody there. That, say other members of staff, is not an uncommon occurrence throughout the rest of the shop.

 37 Eastgate Street

Currently this shop houses the clothing store Next. From 1924 until the 1980s, though, it was the home of Woolworths. And home was an 1892 timber-framed shop boasting four storeys, attics, and a haunted cellar. I was told the following tale by a lady whose brother had worked there. Apparently, every young male assistant who started working at Woolworths was sent on an errand that involved going down into the cellar. This was an initiation ceremony to see if the young men could see the man in black who often walked through the brick wall dividing Woolworths from the building next door. Her brother did. And ran back upstairs very quickly.

 39 Eastgate Street

This eighteenth-century building is home to Sarah, Chester's most famous ghost. Until 2021 it was Thorntons chocolate shop, but the extravagantly decorated facade shows it used to be a treasured house and home.

Stand back and admire the facade. Better still, stop for a cuppa and perhaps a cake to give you time to read through the stories about this shop. There are many.

'Oh, I know all about the ghost at Thorntons,' said the lady on my ghost tour in the spring of 2015. 'I used to work in the job centre in Chester and we were always sending new staff there – people got so spooked by all the goings-on.'

Despite the manager at Thorntons insisting that no recent member of staff had ever seen or heard a ghost in the building, Sarah is Chester's most famous – and very active – poltergeist, since she killed herself after assuming she had been jilted on her wedding day. The room where she sat waiting for her fiancé to take her to church was, for the last few decades, a storeroom and Bewley's, tenants of the building before Thorntons, would often find stock moved around in it.

A list of ghost activity in the last few years includes previous Thorntons staff feeling the need to go up the stairs in pairs rather than alone because of an oppressive atmosphere; a member of staff feeling a hand push her; an American lady being pushed roughly in the back after saying

there were no such things as ghosts; and a Thorntons driver refusing to go into the shop because of the atmosphere he felt. Staff also sometimes smelled cigar smoke in the shop when they opened the door in the morning.

I was passing Thorntons late

one evening and stopped to talk to the delivery driver who was unloading his van with another colleague, before they transferred it to the Thorntons store in the cellar. He said other drivers had warned him about the ghost activity at Thorntons but he had just laughed it off. So, the first time he made a delivery there, he and his colleague adopted their usual routine of his colleague unloading the goods from the van into the shop while he took them down into the cellar and stored them on the shelves. While he was working down there alone, however, he distinctly heard someone saying hello to him, even using his name. He turned round quickly but the cellar was empty. Since then, they have adopted their current practice of doing each stage together.

Most of the poltergeist activity is in either the cellar or the upstairs room where Sarah hanged herself. An electrician working in the cellar, though, was convinced he was being watched. And there is the tale of a burglar who was so terrified of what he saw down there that he ran out of the building, taking nothing with him. Not even his set of tools with his fingerprints clearly on them! Guides and customers have seen lights on the top floor going on and off during ghost tours in the evening, and one couple on a tour saw a lady wearing a light-coloured dress looking out of the upstairs window.

Until a decade ago, Sarah had only misbehaved once on the shop floor, and that was on the first Valentine's Day after Thorntons had moved into the building. The manager locked up the shop on 13 February, leaving a beautiful display in the window. When she returned the next morning, the display had been completely destroyed. Obviously, Sarah did not want anyone else enjoying a romantic moment if she had been denied hers!

In the past few years, though, Sarah has started joining in ghost tours. The first incident was in autumn 2012. A ghost guide was with a group in front of the shop window. He had just said that Sarah never came downstairs into the shop when a box of chocolates fell off the display in the window. That was the end of the tour, as all the shocked customers got out their cameras.

A few months later, another guide had just finished telling the story of Sarah, when one of the men in the group said he was a freezer engineer and he had just witnessed something that could not possibly happen: while the guide was talking, the temperature gauge on the ice cream freezer in the window went up; when she stopped talking, it went down. The same thing happened so regularly to me that summer that I went into the shop to enquire if there was a problem with the freezer: there was not. Could the temperature possibly change so quickly? It could not and did not, I was told. But the thermometer continued to tell a different story.

The following Hallowe'en, I was in front of the window when my tour group noticed that the decorations had slowly but clearly started to revolve, whereas at first everything had been perfectly still. That happened regularly from then on, until the closure of Thorntons. After the first time, I went to check and there were no air currents around the walls or ceiling that could

cause them to move. In
February 2014, another
ghost group noticed
a box of chocolates
in the middle of the
floor. It was too far
from the shelves to
have fallen off and
it is inconceivable a
member of staff would
have stepped over it
and left it there on their
way out at the end
of the day. The ghost
guides were thrilled that
Sarah was joining in the

tours, and were glad she was finally getting some reward for
what she suffered all those years ago.

However, in June 2015 I had a very strange experience,
which could explain a lot of the ghost activity at Thorntons. I
was conducting a tour for a group of international business
people and stopped in front of Thorntons to tell my story. As
usual, I was facing my group while they were looking at the
shopfront and me. Soon after I started talking, a Swedish lady
interrupted to ask questions about Sarah. Where did she die?
We believe she died either down in the cellar or up in her first-
floor bedroom, I replied, as that is where the poltergeist activity
is. No, she corrected me, she died up in her bedroom. How did
she die? We believe she was hanged, I replied. The Swedish
lady nodded in agreement. When she then asked what colour
hair Sarah had, I asked the lady if she had anything she wanted
to tell me. I will speak to you after the tour, she said: she

explained later that she did not want to give details at that point in front of her colleagues because she was concerned it might affect her standing in the group.

The Swedish lady introduced herself as Sophia and said that she had psychic powers but was reluctant to use them. However, when she meets a ghost it is usually because they want her help, and they give her no peace until she provides it. When the group had arrived at Thorntons, she had immediately seen Sarah in the front of the shop. Sarah had brown hair parted in the middle and loosely tied back in a bun. She was wearing a pale yellow, silky dress with puff sleeves. She had a noose around her neck and was pleading with Sophia to help her move on but her voice was very sore and raspy because of the rope.

Sophia said that all the activity in the shop during ghost tours was Sarah's way of asking for help: indeed, while we were in front of the shop that evening the temperature of the freezer had dropped from -14°C to -18°C. Sophia would have to help Sarah move on very soon, she said, or she would follow her back to Sweden. After returning to Sweden, Sophia wrote as promised and I copy her email here, with her permission:

Dear Mary Ann, I promised to get back to you about Sarah and tell you about the story she 'showed me' … Sarah was engaged to get married to Wilhelm. Just before the wedding day he was shot by a pistol, murdered. In the house where Sarah lived, there also lived another man with a connection to Sarah. He could be her father, or another tenant in the house or the owner. He strongly rejected the thought of her getting married and wanted to prevent it. Did he shoot Wilhelm? I don't know. Sarah died hanging from a thick rope, probably on the second floor. And somehow this man was responsible for her death. As a spirit Sarah was aware that she was dead but chose not to move on. Why?

Because Wilhelm was still out there searching for her not accepting or understanding his own death. I believe that time was ending for Sarah to help Wilhelm over to the light. They were in different dimensions and Sarah could not communicate with him and he couldn't see or hear her at all. I was the link she needed to make them communicate. The other man was stuck in the cellar/basement. And could not move over to the other side either as long as Sarah was still there. I helped Sarah and Wilhelm over the same night as our ghost tour, and the other man the night after.

On my last evening, I went to the shop to check it. Sarah was no longer there, but just outside the door, on the step, there were strange energies. Almost like an opening to another dimension. I tried to close it when I came back to Sweden but I'm not sure I succeeded. I've tried to draw Sarah, Wilhelm and the other man from my memory just to show you. Sarah had brown hair and eyes and a light yellow silky dress. Wilhelm was blond with curly hair and his jacket was blue. The other man was wearing something in leather. I believe they lived in early 1800 or late 1700.

I suspect that even the most hardened sceptic would be intrigued by that story. For example, is the man trapped in the cellar the one who is seen going through the wall into the old Woolworths shop cellar?

I, meanwhile, was concerned that Chester had lost its most famous ghost and a popular tourist attraction. I need not have worried. A week later I returned with another ghost tour group, and once again we witnessed the temperature of the freezer falling.

Some time later, a member of my ghost tour took photographs from our position opposite Thorntons, just as a man was walking past the shop. We were intrigued when the man suddenly turned his head and looked through Thorntons window as he passed. Then we looked at the photos and enlarged one of them to focus on where he was looking, to see what had startled him. There, very clearly at the back of the shop, was the shadow of a woman.

Sarah may be at rest but Chester's ghost tours are safe!

6 The Eastgate

Legend has it that if three old crones are seen waiting at the Eastgate, there will be a national tragedy. Apparently, on the afternoon of 30 August 1997, a couple who were out shopping noticed three old ladies who were visibly upset. When they asked what the matter was, the ladies said the Princess of Wales had been killed in a car accident. Ten hours later, news of the fatal accident was reported in the media. Who were the old ladies, and how did they know what was going to happen?

Now it is the time of night
That the graves, all gaping wide,
Every one lets forth his sprite
In the church-way paths to glide ...

William Shakespeare,
A Midsummer Night's Dream

Watergate Street Area

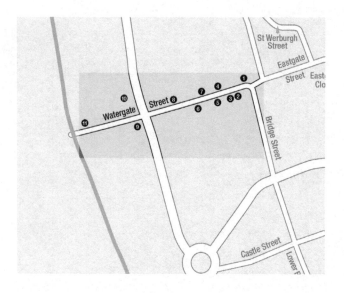

As the name suggests, Watergate Street used to lead to Chester's thriving port area. Chester was the major port in the north-west from Roman times until the nineteenth century, when the river finally silted up too much to allow merchant shipping to come right up to the port. Even until the end of the sixteenth century, you would get your feet wet if you walked more than a few steps past the Watergate. However, wharves, docks and shipping moved further and further north as the river narrowed and the road eventually was able to continue through the Watergate onto new, reclaimed land.

Watergate Street Area

The medieval gate itself had a very small arched entrance, suitable for stopping people as they came into the city and extracting taxes on goods they were bringing in from the ships. The Earl of Derby, head of the Stanley family, found his ownership of the Sergeancy of the Watergate very lucrative, but by the end of the eighteenth century income had fallen dramatically. The Watergate was therefore sold to the city, who replaced it in 1778 with the red sandstone arch that is there today.

In the Roman fortress, Watergate Street was half of the Via Principalis, the main road that crossed the fortress. From that period until the demise of shipping in Chester, Watergate Street was its busiest area, with goods coming into the city being stored in the warehousing here and sold in its many shops. In the late eighteenth century there was, therefore, quite a lot of rebuilding and change of usage. The nineteenth century also saw a lot of necessary rebuilding or restoration of the medieval Rows buildings. By the 1960s, though, it was a sad, neglected and crumbling area – the city's quietest. But it is currently becoming lively once again, with bars and cafes towards the Cross and, further down, a developing art quarter with galleries and studios.

As you walk down the street, look up at God's Providence House on the left with its wonderfully ornate plaster facade and timber frame. But do not be fooled by the date 1652, carved into the beam on either side of the upstairs: this was a complete rebuild in 1862 but, to the delight of the newly formed Archaeological Society at that time, it was rebuilt as a complete copy of the original. The inscription on the main beam, *God's Providence is Mine Inheritance*, gave the original house its name and thanked God for sparing the family in the house at that time from the plague.

Further down the street you will notice Watergate Row North disappears. The Row here was enclosed in the early nineteenth century but the steep steps up to the front doors indicate their previous history.

Watergate Street has had a long and varied history, so it is understandable that there is a lot of ghost activity here. And as much of its history is related to its maritime links, it is hardly surprising that one of the first ghosts you might meet is a sailor wandering up and down the street looking for his shipmates.

 ## 2 Watergate Street

There has been a pub on the site of The Victoria since the thirteenth century, but it was obviously thought politic to rename the pub in the mid-nineteenth century, when Victoria ascended to the throne. The pub has a Victorian interior with lovely fireplaces but it carries the sad tale of a young boy who burnt to death. At some point in the nineteenth century it was the young boy's job to put wood on the fire when necessary. Unfortunately, one day he stumbled as he was doing his job, fell into the fire, and burned to death. From time to time he can be seen once again re-enacting his horrible death.

There is also, according to old tales, a ghost in the cellar, but nobody has seen him recently. Instead, there are constant stories of people being tapped on the shoulder or feeling that someone

is brushing past them. In 2014 an employee working alone in the office heard the gasp of a shocked woman.

2 11 Watergate Street

Watergate's Wine Bar considers itself to be housed in the oldest undercroft in the whole of Chester. It can certainly lay claim to be the oldest: although it

has a nineteenth-century frontage, it has two vaulted sandstone naves as well as a simpler one: the staff refer to them as tunnels and they are supposed to date back to the thirteenth, or even the twelfth, century.

Go down the steps into the pub and admire the wonderful skills of the medieval masons, but keep your eyes open for a sailor, who sits there contemplating his beer rather than the centuries-old architecture, as he waits for his shipmates to join him.

According to staff, in recent years there has also been a considerable amount of poltergeist activity by, they believe, a little girl. And in 2001, staff were clearing and cleaning the tunnels after the wine bar had closed. One of the members of staff had brought his dog to work and he was sitting quietly at the entrance to the first tunnel while his owner and his colleagues worked systematically in tunnel one, then tunnel two. When they then moved to tunnel three, however, they heard the dog barking, seemingly petrified. They all ran back to the poor dog, who was shaking. And staring at all the chairs, which had been thrown from on top of the tables onto the floor.

3   19 Watergate Street

The Weasel and Bug is sandwiched between the two entrances to 21 Watergate Street, another stunningly vaulted building, originally two separate undercrofts. When the two medieval shops were made into one, it appears that the shop, now occupied by the Weasel and Bug, was created to make use of excess frontage space.

The owner of the Weasel and Bug, a delightful children's toy shop, moved into the building in the summer of 2017 and, being security conscious, immediately installed CCTV that could be watched remotely. The very first time she checked the cameras when she was at home, however, she saw poltergeist activity and a small child playing in a corner of the shop. The owner had good reason to check: she was already aware of things being moved while the shop was closed and empty, especially in the storeroom in the cellar.

That summer, a young girl who used to work in the shop would often sit at the top of the stairs leading to the cellar when the shop was quiet. One day while she was sitting there, she saw the ghost of a boy walking past the bottom of the stairs.

Two days later, she joked with the owner that perhaps they ought to give him a name, and she chose the name George. The next day, when the owner arrived to open up the shop, she found the name WILBUR had been spelled out with wooden letters on the play table at the front of the shop. The young boy was obviously determined to put the shop assistant right.

The poltergeist activity continues. In June 2020, the owner's mother was in the cellar tidying and cleaning but her duster, polish and scissors kept being moved. More annoyingly, items ordered by customers and awaiting collection keep being moved and turn up some time later somewhere totally random, for example in the lavatory or among the Christmas decorations. The owner finds it extremely annoying and embarrassing, as she has to apologise to the buyers and explain their purchases are bound to turn up somewhere in the shop at some point. When I last spoke to the owner, in July 2020, two items of clothing had disappeared. And they were still looking for them …

 26 Watergate Row North

This building upon the Row, up on the right side of the street, is home to Crichtons, a bespoke men's tailor shop. It is also the home of something unidentified, too, according to staff. They often hear noises in the cellar, but when they open the cellar door, the noises immediately stop.

 17 Watergate Row South

Leche House, nearly opposite Crichtons on Watergate Row South, was occupied until recently by The Sofa Workshop, but was once owned by John Leche, Edward III's doctor. The Leche family continued to live there until the seventeenth century, when the facade was moved further into the street. The sash windows are eighteenth century, the timber frame is fifteenth century, and the undercroft below is fourteenth century: Leche House is, in fact, a glorious and beautiful jigsaw of a building, like many in the city. What is unique here, though, is the original medieval great hall with a huge fireplace that has a priest hole accessed from the top right-hand corner.

It is believed that Catherine of Aragon stayed here when she came to Chester with her first husband, Henry VIII's brother, Prince Arthur. Is she the sad figure who sometimes looks down from the upstairs window overlooking Watergate Street?

The staff at The Sofa Workshop used to love working at Leche House but they did find it dark and creepy late at night, even though there have been no ghostly experiences for some time. Even a séance about fifteen years ago revealed nothing. However, there are supposed to be two ghosts in this building besides that of the sad lady: the ghosts of a young seventeenth-century girl and a monk.

6 **51/53 Watergate Row**

Bishop Lloyd's Palace is a beautiful seventeenth-century building, both inside and out, on Watergate Row East. On the exterior are wooden carvings depicting Old Testament scenes and also a coat of arms showing the three legs of the Isle of Man, a reminder that Bishop Lloyd was Bishop of Sodor and Man before he became Bishop of Chester in 1605. Bishop

Lloyd's palace is rarely open to the public but is well worth a visit, if you can, to admire the two wonderful reception rooms with superb plaster ceilings and an ornate Jacobean chimney breast.

Keep an eye open, though – a man has been seen walking through a wall, and an American tourist in the palace once felt a cold hand on her neck.

7 38–42 Watergate Street

Katie's Tearooms look like two separate buildings but were originally just one large medieval stone house. You enter into a small tea room at street level but the first-floor restaurant was actually a medieval great hall, which was made into four rooms in the late sixteenth century. On the second floor there is more restaurant seating space, but in medieval times it was divided into a bustling hub of offices and shops.

One day a lady was seated at a table in the ground-floor restaurant, near a young couple. When the couple finished their meal and left the restaurant, the lady followed them and stopped them: she wanted to warn them that they were being followed by a sad man, obviously a ghost as the lady was the only person who could see him. However, the girl recognised him from the lady's description: he had been her previous boyfriend who had committed suicide. The lady saw the couple again in Liverpool some time later. The sad man was still following them.

None of the current staff members have seen any ghosts, but customers have from time to time reported sightings in the upper rooms.

8 28–34 Watergate Street

Booth Mansion is a beautifully elegant building that is clearly visible from Eastgate Street: George Booth deemed it worthwhile to pay the £10 fine he was given for building his mansion at an angle to the street, because it meant it could be seen and admired from a great distance. The mansion is actually two thirteenth-century houses, simply given a new facade by Booth in 1700 but keeping the original medieval staircase to the first floor. This staircase leads to Booth's ballroom, which soon became a popular social centre for the elite of Chester.

In autumn 2006, Booth Mansion reopened as a tea room and restaurant. During the renovations and just before it opened, the owner had a dream where her father, who had died some years previously, had completed all the necessary repairs and was relaxing in an armchair in the corner of the ballroom. From that moment, the owner felt the ballroom had a lovely peaceful atmosphere, despite hearing the stories of ghost activity from an electrician who had worked there previously.

9 83 Watergate Street

Stanley Palace is on the other side of the busy inner ring road, which cuts across Watergate Street, leaving a short stretch to descend slowly to the Watergate. The land in this area was owned by the Black Friary, one of Chester's monasteries until the dissolution of the monasteries by Henry VIII in the 1530s. The land was then sold to Sir Peter Warburton, MP for Chester, who built the Elizabethan black-and-white timber-framed building that still stands there in 1591. When Sir Peter died, the house was inherited by his daughter, who was married to Sir Thomas Stanley, so the house was renamed Stanley Palace.

Stanley Palace boasts two ghosts. One is a seventeenth-century lady in grey who moves around the main reception rooms. The other is James Stanley, 7th Earl of Derby, a Royalist who was held prisoner there during the Civil War and was executed on a charge of treason in 1651 for his active support of Charles II. He can be seen wandering around the ground floor.

In addition, the secretary of the English Speaking Union, when working alone in an office here, sometimes heard footsteps and voices in the building.

Because of its history, Stanley Palace has often been visited by paranormal investigators. One group stayed overnight there in June 2014, focusing their activities on the hall and staircase where a man was reported to have died. They saw nothing that night, but when they replayed the video footage, three figures could clearly be seen on the staircase. Close examination shows them to be probably children. They had never been seen before, nor have they been seen since, and nobody has any idea who they are.

10 Stanley Place

Opposite Stanley Palace is Stanley Street, which leads to the beautiful Stanley Place. This quiet corner of Chester has a cobbled street lined with lovely Georgian houses that are now occupied by an English Language School, part of the Queen's School, various consultancies, and some private housing. I was told about the ghost activity in one of the houses in Stanley Square in the summer of 2018 by a young couple who lived in the ground-floor flat. For obvious reasons, I will not give the

number of the house. The occupier told me how one morning he woke up at 3 a.m. and heard a man say, 'Hello, welcome.' There was no one there. Three months later, his girlfriend heard a woman whispering 'Hello' in her ear.

As the house is divided into flats, the residents are very security conscious, but sometimes the couple find the doors to the basement open. They never find anyone down there. And only the caretaker has the key.

One night they were both woken at 4 a.m. by someone walking backwards and forwards very slowly on the cobbles near their window. This continued for an hour. The walker had shoes with heels that made a 'clickety' sound. 'Did you have a look outside the window?' I asked. Not a chance! They were too scared and pulled the duvet over their heads to try and hide the sound on the cobbles.

11 102 Watergate Street

This house is one of a row of tall, proud Georgian houses that stretch from the corner of Stanley Street to the Watergate. No.102 Watergate Street has nothing to make it stand out from the others in the street, but not many people would care to live there, given its history of poltergeist activity. For many years before the Second World War, the house was used by the army's Western Command. Staff often heard noises in the upstairs rooms, but one night in 1937 the two soldiers on duty on the ground floor heard a loud crash and something heavy being dragged across the floor above. They investigated and found nothing but an empty room.

Now I know what a ghost is.
Unfinished business, that's what.

Salman Rushdie,
The Satanic Verses

Bridge Street Area

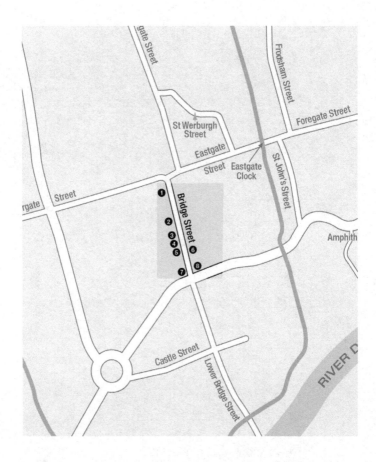

Bridge Street stretches from the very centre of Chester, at St Peter's Church, to St Michael's Church at the junctions of Pepper Street, Grosvenor Street and Lower Bridge Street.

When Chester was the Roman Fortress Deva, Bridge Street was the Via Praetoria, leading from the Porta Pretoria, where the traffic lights at the junction are now situated. Whereas the Via Principalis was one straight line east–west through the fortress, the Via Praetoria stopped in front of the Principia, which, as the centre of administration and representing the power of the Empire, dominated the fortress and needed to be treated with respect, not passed by in a rush to the barracks on the north side of the fortress. The north–south route still has the dogtooth junction, which the soldiers had to take to walk up the side of the Principia.

St Peter's Church now stands on this site. It was restored by John Douglas in the late nineteenth century, when the whole city centre seems to have been rebuilt: if you compare the exterior walls of the church at the front and at the side, you will see why restoration in Chester was an urgent necessity in the nineteenth century. Inside the church is evidence of its long history: a medieval wall painting, a fifteenth-century brass, a seventeenth-century font and nineteenth-century stained-glass windows.

In front of St Peter's is the Cross, also known as the High Cross, which marks the very centre of Chester. The Cross has stood here since the fifteenth century and from here the town crier would issue his daily news. David Mitchell, the current Town Crier, still does, at 12 noon every day during the summer months. During the Civil War, however, the Cross was smashed by the Roundheads, and it was not put back together and reinstated until Chester became pedestrianised in 1975.

Most of the buildings that face St Peter's were replaced in the second half of the nineteenth century by the glorious black-and-white buildings that still enhance the city, replacing the crumbling dilapidated buildings that Louise Rayner so vividly painted in the 1840s. Examples of her paintings of Chester can be seen in the Grosvenor Museum.

Bridge Street is a delightful mishmash of buildings, no two looking alike, not one exactly what it seems. Further down on the left, for example, is St Michael's Row, leading to St Michael's Arcade. It was opened in 1910 with great fanfare by the Duke of Westminster, the owner, but with mounting horror and howls of complaints from the good citizens of Chester. The whole facade was covered in pale Royal Doulton tiles. Now, these look very elegant in the sophisticated Edwardian St Michael's Arcade, where they were allowed to stay, but totally unacceptable outside facing Bridge Street. A year later, with less fanfare, they had been replaced by the current, much more acceptable, black-and-white frontage. One or two shops still have Roman ruins in their basements, the remains of Fortress Deva's bath house which was sited there.

12 Bridge Street

Thomas Cowper House at 12 Bridge Street is another example of a building with a mixed heritage. After the Civil War, Thomas Cowper, Mayor of Chester during the siege, had enough money to quickly repair the war-damaged frontage with the most readily available material, wood. The year, 1664, is proudly carved into the decorated facade. At the rear of the ground-floor shop, though, there is still the original early fourteenth-century undercroft, the only one in Chester with a staircase linking the street level and the Row level of the building. It now forms part of the fire safety system of the building: if there is a fire on the Row level, staff should escape down it; if there is a fire on the street level, staff should escape up it. However, staff have been reluctant to go anywhere near the stairs, let alone go up them, in the past. After my experience in March 2015, it is not surprising.

At that time, the building was occupied by the Viyella/CC dress shop. In 2015, I went in to ask questions as part of my research for the first edition of *Chester City of Ghosts*. When the Viyella/CC staff explained how they refused to use the medieval staircase, I asked if I could go up it. As I unbolted the door to the staircase, a cloud flew into the air from the bolt, too big and too light to be accumulated dust. The member of staff who was with me recoiled a few steps. I opened the door, looked up the flight of stone steps and took a photo – at which point my camera went out of control, taking more than a dozen photos in quick succession. I decided to abandon my plan of going up the steps because by this time my scalp had begun to itch very uncomfortably, just as it had in the Bluecoat School at the Northgate. This itching continued until I finally had to leave

the shop, by which time the assistants had told me of all the other ghostly activity: clothes hangers being rattled; doors banging upstairs. As for the boy who is supposed to haunt the shop after dying as a result of a fall in the undercroft in Victorian times, staff have seen and heard nothing. But the succession of photos my camera took seem to show a man standing on the stairs.

Viyella/CC was replaced by Trespass, an outdoor clothing store. Soon after they had moved in, I popped in to ask if they had experienced any ghost activity. They most certainly had. When they took over the premises, they had installed motion-sensor CCTV cameras on the street-level entrance door, the Row-level entrance door and the top of the medieval stairs at the back of the shop. Every time someone walked too close to the two outer doors, the camera would record it. However, the camera at the top of the medieval stairs was also triggered a number of times but there was never anyone visible on the video.

Both shops were very welcoming if I asked to bring small groups of people to walk up the haunted medieval staircase. In July 2017, a group of American tourists braved the stairs, and the last person in the group took photos of his wife who was walking up just in front of him. Outside the shop, when he showed the group the photos, we could see a big ball of yellow light hovering under his wife's foot. The photo he took from the top of the empty stairs showed the ball of yellow light having moved to near the side wall. The shop's light on the stairs, however, was a white LED lamp.

One night in 2019, I was unable to complete my ghost tour with my final story at this shop because two police officers were guarding the entrance to it. The glass entrance door lay shattered into hundreds of small pieces on the floor behind them. 'Who broke it?' I asked. And there was the problem. The whole incident had been caught on Chester's CCTV and there was not a single person near the shop when the glass door smashed.

2 22 Bridge Street Row West

Up on Bridge Street Row West, further down from the Thomas Cowper House, is Suzie K @ The Secret Garden, a fascinating shop that used to be called Sally's Secret Garden.

The shop has more than one secret, including a magnificently ornate Carolean ceiling dating from the 1670s in its upstairs cafe. Both Sally and Suzie have seen frequent ghost activity, some of it even caught on CCTV.

In February 2015, someone attending a Wiccan workshop there said they had seen a boy, about 10 years old, running around upstairs and playing with a cup and ball. This explains a lot – especially how two large paintings, which were leaning back against a wall in the upstairs art gallery, were caught on camera suddenly and simultaneously falling to the floor. It possibly also explains the poltergeist activity while Sally owned the shop: items on display in the shop were moved during the night; large items went missing and then reappeared in strange places, such as the lavatory; doors opened and closed upstairs when nobody was there. A young man in the shop had his hair tugged as he admired some jewellery. And a lady in the therapy room heard a little boy crying. When she tried to move away, he kicked her chair.

The boy is not alone, though: upstairs in the cafe there are two ghosts who can make people feel ill. There is the ghost of a monk in the corner by the window, who makes people short of breath if they invade his body space. And I started feeling severe chest pains when I was sitting in the far corner of the room but they stopped as soon as I left the shop. This is where, I was told, a Dutch sea captain who had owned the building previously had died of a chest infection. The husband of Suzy, the new owner, often smelled strong pipe smoke in this room in the first few months of 2020, while the shop was closed to customers. Is this the sea captain enjoying the peace and quiet?

Suzy has frequently seen a man in a greatcoat, a warm winter coat, standing on the upstairs landing, just watching her; her assistant has seen the same man in the upstairs cafe area. This man is also visible to a medium who visits the shop and has been seen by quite a few people who meet as a group in the Carolean room.

The strangest experience, though, was caught on the shop's CCTV camera in October 2014. There are four security cameras (two downstairs and two upstairs) with a monitor screen near the till at the front of the shop. One evening, all the lights had been turned off and Sally's husband was waiting for her near the till when he noticed a ball of miasma on the screen that appeared to be moving around and above his head. The ball was invisible in the shop and could not have been caused by any reflected light because the shop was in darkness. Sally and her husband then spent twenty minutes watching and playing with the ball – when they tried to touch it, it would move away, slowly in Sally's case but violently if her husband attempted to reach it. This was the only time they had noticed a ball of miasma in the shop area, but it happened often in the art gallery upstairs when Sally's husband was there – that, too, had been captured on CCTV. Obviously, someone did not like him. Perhaps it is the ghost of the lady who died falling down the stairs many years ago. In the 1930s a medium was called to the house because the then owner, Mrs Dudley, was woken every night by footsteps continually going up the steps to her bedroom. The medium explained they were caused by the lady who wanted to explain that her death was not accidental, as assumed at the time – her husband had pushed her down the stairs. Perhaps Sally's husband looked like the wicked husband!

A few weeks before Sally left the shop, she told me how two ladies, on separate occasions, had seen a lady dressed in black walking down the stairs. Of course, I could not then resist going into the shop wearing my ghost outfit of black hat, black coat, black boots, black gloves and even black lipstick, to be photographed coming down the stairs. Later, Sally contacted me: after I left, the computer and the CCTV cameras stopped working for the rest of the day. Since then, some customers have felt they were being pushed down the stairs and have had to move down more quickly than they intended.

The ghosts are getting more and more active now, as they have got used to the new owner, Suzie. Like Sally, she has also felt short of breath sometimes when in the front corner of the upstairs cafe. Not all the time, though, because the monk has now apparently decided to go wandering: he has been seen by a customer near the door to the Secret Garden.

A female ghost is now often on the ground floor of the shop. Suzie can feel her walking past and the assistant has felt her stroking her hair. Another member of staff has felt someone walk through her and then stroke her hair. One customer felt someone touch her head, another has felt someone press her arm. This ghost is obviously a gentle presence.

The little boy is still playing his usual tricks: the door to the private staff area upstairs is often open in the mornings, even though it is always firmly closed at night because of the alarm system. An assistant has seen him running across the landing. Another member of staff heard running footsteps at the back of the shop, saw the boy standing by the cake stands, and thought he was a customer's child. The boy smiled at her. He was wearing old-fashioned breeches, a peaked hat and a waistcoat, so she thought he had dressed up for a school story day. She asked him where his mummy was, turned to look in the shop and saw no one, turned back again and the boy had disappeared. He is fond of nudging people, tapping them on the arm, as they browse in the shop, including trying to squeeze between the legs of one customer. And just as he did with Sally, the little boy is still moving things around the shop, including chairs, boxes and items from Suzy's shopping bag. The ghosts are obviously very happy with the new owner of the Secret Garden. In the spring of 2021, though, Suzie extended her shop to street level. It will be interesting to see if the ghosts follow her downstairs.

3 28 Bridge Street

This Grade II listed building was a pub from 1789 until 2002. Standing on the corner of Bridge Street and Commonhall Street, Ye Olde Vaults was run by George Barlow, a man with very high standards. From time to time, if he feels disgruntled with what is going on in the building even now, he will move things around and throw things off shelves, especially in the upstairs rooms. Apparently there is a cold, threatening atmosphere in the cellar and a man in a top hat has been seen, possibly the ghost of a sixteenth-century traveller who hanged himself there.

The occupants until 2020, Sta Travel, experienced no ghostly activity. However, one of Chester's tour guides had personal experience, as he lived there when his father was a publican. This guide does not believe in ghosts, definitely does not – but one morning he was too afraid to get out of bed because he had heard a noise by the door and had felt the presence of something evil. In the cellar there was an old, heavy wooden door that was always jammed open, but one day it slammed shut and the guide needed help to push it open again. On another occasion, he and customers were talking in the bar about how George used to bottle his own whisky when, suddenly, there was a noise. A plastic optic label had fallen off to reveal another underneath, labelled George Barlow Highland Brand Scotch Whisky. There was nobody behind the bar at the time!

4 32 Bridge Street

Until 2018, the restaurant Urbano was at street level, with Liberty Bell, a craft shop, above it on the Row. When Liberty Bell left, Urbano took over the Row-level space but had to undertake four months of repairs because of fire damage caused by the air conditioning. During this time, when a workman was busy in the Row-level area, he saw someone walk past him and assumed it was his colleague. His colleague, however, was downstairs. Later, his colleague was working in the same area and could feel someone walking around, although he could see no one.

36 Bridge Street

Côte Brasserie occupies another building with a lovely fourteenth-century arched undercroft at the rear of the street level. There are no old stories of ghosts here, but when I left 12 Bridge Street after my unnerving ghostly experience there in 2015, I came here because it was then Christie's linen shop. I just wanted, I told them, to go into a building that was not haunted and buy something nice. 'What makes you think we have no ghosts?' they replied, and then began to tell their tales.

Firstly, there was often a strong smell of pipe smoke in the corner of the arch. A previous manager had seen a man on the stairs in the stockroom; other members of staff had seen a man hanging by the neck at the back of the shop. The then manager had seen someone sitting in a chair and later saw dents in the cushions; in February 2015, as she opened up the shop, she had felt a presence, as she often did, and heard footsteps.

In the stockroom, which was above the Row level, staff constantly felt that someone was behind them, and often they felt that they were being stopped from going or down the stairs. One visiting member of staff thought this was ridiculous and went up the stairs to the stockroom with no problem, but later had to call for help because she felt unable to get down the stairs.

In 2017, Côte Brasserie moved into the building and there was a staff meeting in the Row-level restaurant before it opened. As the meeting progressed, four or five bottles calmly slid from the shelf onto the floor. Not one of the bottles broke, the shelf was stable and there was no one near. Since then, the harassed kitchen staff have had to cope with frequent ghost activity in the Row-level kitchen, as well as catering for a very busy restaurant. They constantly feel there is someone with them, even when all the other staff have left.

Côte Brasserie has four managers. One of them often hears someone calling his name when he is alone in the restaurant. And early in 2019, two managers were on the ground floor, counting the daily takings after the restaurant had closed. They both suddenly noticed on the CCTV a white light in the fourteenth-century section at the rear of the room. It had the shape and form of a human.

I was told by one manager that lights in the restaurant go on and off all the time. 'Well, that's not surprising, given the age of the building,' I responded. The manager was adamant it was nothing to do with the fuses or electrical circuits – they had been checked the previous month when the lights in the whole building repeatedly went on and off for a whole day. If it were an electrical fault, the manager explained, the lights would go off and stay off; if it were a faulty fuse, all the lights in one fuse section would fail. But there is never a logical explanation for the lights' behaviour.

6 49 Bridge Street Row East

You would often find me in The Mad Hatter's Tea Room, until it sadly had to close down in June 2020 because of the financial effects of the pandemic that year. It was my favourite tea room, in a lovely building with an interesting ghost or two, and I hope the food in the new Italian restaurant, Carbonara, will meet with the resident ghost's approval. The building is seventeenth century and, from 1659 until 1907, it was the vicarage for St Michael's Church at the Cross. It has three floors, with an eighteenth-century staircase leading to the timber-roofed gallery.

The owner of Mad Hatter's told me in 2016 about the lady in grey he would often see on the stairs. But the most active ghost in the building has been a gentleman called

George, who is a poltergeist. That year the manager found tea leaves scattered on the storeroom floor. When she returned to clear them up, she found they had been arranged in the shape of a sausage. She left to tell a colleague and when they returned, the leaves were in the shape of an aeroplane. Again, they left to tell another colleague and when they all returned this time, the leaves were in the shape of a flower. Finally, the manager swept them up.

One morning in May of that year, the owner felt a freezing hand on his throat as he went to unlock the shop door. As soon as he opened it, the hand released its grip and the owner felt a sudden rush of air pass him, as though everyone inside had run to hide. Early in 2020, I was told there had been banging noises by the till at the front of the shop a few times, followed by the customers' bell ringing. There was never anyone there. Perhaps George was still annoyed with the reorganisation in 2018 of the entrance to the shop, with the till being moved from the centre to near the shop door. When that first happened, George spent a few days throwing the hats off the hat stand onto the floor. As soon as staff replaced them, off they would come again.

In March 2020, just before Mad Hatter's, as well as every other restaurant and pub in the country, had to close, the owner had been hoovering the top staircase before the restaurant opened. He put the hoover attachment he had been using on the stairs while he carried the hoover up to the top floor. When he returned, the attachment was missing. He found it later in the storeroom. The only other staff in the building were busy in the kitchen on the floor below, making scones for the day's customers.

7 44–50 Bridge Street

Towards the bottom of Bridge Street, on the right-hand side, is what is reputed to be the oldest shopfront in England. Above the three arches at Row level is the date 1274 AD, and the building itself dates back to the thirteenth century so there may be some truth in the claim. From the 1960s until 1999, the department store

Owen Owen occupied the whole building, and it is there that these two ghost stories happened, both told to me by different ladies who had worked there.

The first lady told how she went to the lavatory just before she unlocked the door to let customers in. When she came back onto the shop floor, a lady in a 1930s suit walked past her into the back and disappeared. The door was still locked.

The second lady was in the wine section of Owen Owen at 8.50 a.m. one day, checking all was in order on the shelves before the shop was opened for business. When she turned back to the counter, she saw a lady waiting to be served. The lady asked for a particular bottle of wine, the assistant turned round to reach for it – and when she turned back to hand it to the customer, she had disappeared. That is when the assistant realised the shop doors were still locked.

8 St Michael's Church

There has been a church on this site since before 1180 but what is visible today is a mid-nineteenth-century rebuild, with parts inside dating back to the fifteenth century. In 1975 it became Chester's History and Heritage Centre, and now houses an exhibition called 'Sick to Death'.

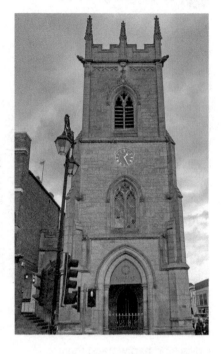

One day a historian working for the Chester City Council was up in the church tower, examining some maps, when she suddenly felt as though there was an evil presence behind her, wanting to harm her. 'I deal with facts and history,' she said, 'not unexplained feelings.' But she came down the stairs as quickly as she could and never went back up there.

In 2019 I was told that a ghost had previously said 'Goodbye' to one of the assistants as she locked up and left. Perhaps it was the man in grey who wears a top hat that a few members of staff have seen.

The murdered do haunt their murderers, I believe.
I know that ghosts have wandered on earth. Be
with me always – take any form – drive me mad!
Only do not leave me in this abyss, where I cannot
find you!

Emily Brontë,
Wuthering Heights

Lower Bridge Street Area

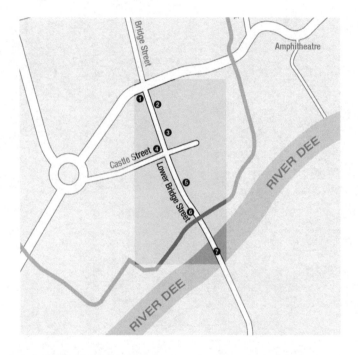

The Lower Bridge Street area is the quarter of Chester that originally lay outside the Roman fortress, and did not become an accepted part of the city itself until the walls were extended down to the river in the twelfth century. It is the area where the Vikings in the ninth century, having tired of attacking Chester, settled down and lived peacefully. The first St Olave's Church to be built on Lower Bridge Street was built for and by these Viking settlers in the twelfth century. The present church is a fifteenth-century replacement; both were named after an eleventh-century Viking king, who managed to achieve sainthood despite behaving like a typical ruthless Viking until he converted to Christianity.

In the Georgian era, Lower Bridge Street was the centre of genteel society, hence the beautiful examples of Georgian houses on both sides of the street. The area went into a steep decline, though, when Grosvenor Bridge was opened in 1831, giving a better route into Wales and removing traffic, trade and prosperity from the area. Fortunately, the powers that be were persuaded to start a restoration scheme for the houses in the 1960s, before they decayed beyond repair.

The Rows on Lower Bridge Street, however, were lost forever. By the late eighteenth century they had all been incorporated into the buildings, apart from number 11, which looks as if it has its own private balcony facing the street. A clue to the previous existence of a Row that has been incorporated into a house on Lower Bridge Street is a set of stairs leading up to the front door of some of them.

The Bridgegate was originally a small, arched entrance, set into a defensive wall that protected Chester from attacks from the south and west. In the early seventeenth century a water tower perched high above it and brought fresh piped water to the citizens of Chester for the first time. The gates would have been firmly locked at night and in times of attack, but in September 1645 they were opened to welcome Charles I to Chester. He stayed at Gamul House, on the right-hand side of Lower Bridge Street, while his army fought the Battle of Rowton Moor. Gamul House is now a pub and restaurant, so you can sit and enjoy a meal next to the fireplace in the stunning interior where Charles would have sat and contemplated his fate after the devastating rout of his army at Rowton Moor.

The Bridgegate was replaced in the 1780s to allow traffic coming over the Old Dee Bridge freer access into the town.

 6 Lower Bridge Street

The Falcon is now a pub, but for centuries it was the town house of the Grosvenor family. Their principal family home is only 4½ miles from Chester but nonetheless it was deemed a bit too exposed to Roundhead attack during the Civil War. The town house inside Chester's defensive city walls seemed a much safer option. (If you are interested in visiting the Duke

of Westminster but are not sure which direction to take, here is a clue: the Falcon is on the corner of Grosvenor Street, which leads to Grosvenor Roundabout, which leads to Grosvenor Bridge, which leads to Grosvenor Road, which leads to Duke's Driveway.)

The first thing Sir Richard Grosvenor did when he moved to Chester was to enclose the Row that ran through his house. It was this act that triggered the enclosure of all but one of the Rows on Lower Bridge Street over the next hundred years. The telltale steps up to the entrance to the pub lead to the bar, where the thirteenth-century pillars bear witness to the deed. Much of the Falcon was remodelled in the sixteenth, seventeenth and nineteenth centuries, but many parts still date back to the original thirteenth-century building and some timbers in the cellar are twelfth century.

The building became a pub in 1778, but was a cocoa house in the late nineteenth century. It is now once again a pub, with a lovely interior. And a poltergeist with good reason to bemoan her fate. There had been no ghost activity for years in the Falcon pub but suddenly, on 15 February 2015, glasses came off the shelves in the bar and both the kettle and the extractor fan in the kitchen turned on in front of a member of staff who was standing nowhere near them.

The ghost who haunts this building is a poltergeist called Molly, a maidservant who was accused of stealing and so was sacked and thrown out of the house by the housekeeper in the middle of the winter. After dying of exposure, she returned to The Falcon to make her presence felt. A previous landlady saw Molly sitting on her bed, but when Molly saw the landlady, she disappeared. Some years ago there was a wedding reception in the upstairs room: all the photos showed a ghostly figure of a female in grey who had definitely not been invited to the wedding.

2 13 Lower Bridge Street

There is a history of things dropping off shelves upstairs in what is now Headmasters hair salon, and there have been reports of an oppressive atmosphere. One manager even heard someone saying goodbye to her as she left the empty shop one evening. But there has been no recent activity, according to the staff of Headmasters.

3 29–31 Lower Bridge Street

Tudor House is an early seventeenth-century building that leans quite alarmingly. Its claim to be Tudor, though, is somewhat questionable. It originally advertised itself as having been built in 1503, but a test on the wooden structure dated it to 1603 or even later. The Tudor dynasty ended with the death of Elizabeth I in 1603.

Nevertheless, it is a lovely building with a Tudor and Georgian facade. And a ghost who seems in no hurry to leave. This is the ghost of a Royalist soldier who was billeted in the top room during the Civil War. One day he leant out of the window to discover the source of the loud noise he had just heard. He realised it was the sound of a cannon being fired when the cannon ball hit him and removed his head. As a Royalist he was, of course, very proud of his appearance, which was now utterly ruined. He can still be heard bemoaning his bad fortune. One lady who worked there in the late 1970s and early 1980s, when the building was a dress shop, heard him frequently. When she went up to his old room, by then a storeroom, she would hear a man talking to her but could never find anyone there.

Another lady, who now works at a local school, worked there as a shop assistant from 1990 to 1991, when it was a casual clothes shop at the front and a record shop at the back. When the lady was first employed in the clothes shop, she was told to ignore any strange events, such as the circular rack of clothes turning, or someone blowing in her ear. Both those things happened frequently, but her patience was sorely tried one morning: the previous afternoon she had sorted and tidied dozens of boxes of shoes in the storeroom before locking up. When she returned the next morning, every box was on the floor, despite the alarm having been on all night.

The man who ran the record shop lived upstairs, and entered the shop by an iron-gated staircase that was only unlocked to give him access. One day the manager found him at the bottom

of the stairs, head in hands, looking very shocked. Seconds earlier, as he was walking down the stairs, he had felt and then seen a woman falling past him. But when he ran down to help her, there was nobody there. The gate was still locked and the alarm was still on in the shop.

4. 48–50 Lower Bridge Street

Ye Olde King's Head is another building where evidence of the enclosed Row is clearly visible on the first floor. The building dates from the early thirteenth century, with modifications in the fifteenth, sixteenth and early seventeenth centuries; the wonderful frontage is mid-seventeenth century.

There are many stories of ghosts linked to the Old King's Head, which is hardly surprising given the number of ghosts prowling its corridors. There is a man, sometimes two men, who appear to ladies sleeping alone in Rooms 4 or 6. They both died as a result of a duel for the hand of a lady who lived there.

There are the ghosts of a mother, her baby and a man in a cape and top hat. There are also a grand total of thirteen visiting ghosts, according to paranormal investigators.

Nobody knows who the other ghosts are, but they certainly make their presence felt. In 2008, a waitress made small talk with a man who was sitting on his bed one morning as she tidied up, but there was no response. When she complained to the rest of the staff about his rudeness, she was told that room had not been used. And when they all went up to check, they found the room was locked.

Later, when the pub changed hands, the new chef began to refuse to come out of the kitchen because he had gone out too many times to see who was walking past the frosted glass in the kitchen, only to find there was nobody there. When the landlady was talking to me on one occasion, she turned her head suddenly because someone had tapped her on the shoulder. I could see nobody behind her. The same landlady had only been in the pub a few weeks when she saw a man in a top hat and cape enter the bar through the middle doorway, cross the room, and silently leave by the back door. She thought it was her husband playing a trick on her because of all the ghost stories they had been told. However, when she followed him out, there was nobody there and her husband was still outside the front door. The landlord himself was regularly woken by the sound of a baby crying, only to find their baby fast asleep. But he could still hear a baby crying.

One story involves a visiting priest at St John the Baptist's Church. In 2012, he booked rooms for a relative from Canada and her son. The lady went to bed while her son went exploring the town. She was somewhat concerned for his safety in a strange town, but was reassured when she heard his footsteps in the corridor and her door rattling. She was less reassured in the morning to learn her son had come nowhere near her room the whole night.

A few years ago, the manager of the Old King's Head showed me a file of stories of ghost activity compiled by people who had experienced it while staying overnight in one of the rooms. The accounts are all similar: being kept awake by noises of children running up and down the corridor, drawers opening and shutting, doors slamming. Each account described how scared the writers had been, but they were really looking forward to coming back again. One couple were so scared they had left their bed in the middle of the night, left the hotel, and slept in the car. But it was such a wonderful experience, they said, that they could not wait to repeat.

5 2 Duke Street

The Cross Keys pub on the corner of Duke Street and Lower Bridge Street is a lovely example of a late Victorian building, although it replaced a pub that had been there since the 1740s. It has no ghosts. And the reason I am so sure is because the landlord told me. He has the ability to see ghosts and regularly used to see two at his previous pub. But he has neither seen nor felt any ghostly presence since he has lived at the Cross Keys.

However, one night a few years after my conversation with the landlord, I was at a concert in one of the upstairs rooms. I had taken the precaution of putting my glass safely out of the way under my chair, as had most of the others in the room. An unnecessary precaution, because everybody was sitting listening to the music. Until, that is, my drink was knocked over during one of the songs, swiftly followed by the glass under the chair of someone in the row behind me. But who was the culprit? We could see no answer.

6 94 Lower Bridge Street

Oh! Ed! Kitchen! Onion!

This is how I was introduced to a very interesting ghost story about the Bear and Billet, the lovely timber-framed building at the bottom of Lower Bridge Street.

The Bear and Billet is one of the last completely tim-ber-framed buildings to be built in the country, which is under-standable given that in 1666, two years after it was built, there was an event that made people more keen on other building techniques: the Great Fire of London. At that time, 1664, the site was owned by the Earl of Shrewsbury, who had the sergeancy of the Bridgegate, a very lucrative post. He was therefore able to rebuild his previous house very quickly after it suffered irreparable damage from cannon fire during the Civil War. The result was the splendid building that exists to this day, with its hundreds of tiny windows.

John Lennon's grand-mother was born here in 1873, but it is not her ghost which is reputed to haunt the Bear and Billet. It is that of a young girl who can be heard crying in an upstairs room or seen standing on the stairs. Many years ago, when the Earl of Shrews-bury lived there, he locked her in an upstairs room with no food or water as a punishment, and then promptly rode off to Shrewsbury for a few days and forgot all about her plight. She cried for help, food and water, but the other servants were too scared of the Earl to go against his orders. By the time he returned, she was dead.

The ghost has a sense of humour, though, despite her fate: the landlady and other members of staff often have trouble finding things because they have been moved, only for them to turn up later in the original place. It is something they have all come to expect. Bottles and glasses behind the bar frequently fall off the shelf and smash on the floor for no visible reason.

The landlady and her family keep their shoes on a shoe rack at the bottom of the stairs leading from the second floor to the staff accommodation. Sadly, her father died some time ago, but the family forgot to remove his leather slippers from the shoe rack. A few months after his death, his slippers moved during the night from the shoe rack to the top of the stairs.

In the flat, the doors are heavy and the floors uneven, so the doors stick but, nonetheless, in the early hours of the morning the landlady is often woken by the sound of doors opening and being slammed shut.

The landlady has a dog, which will often sit and stare at one particular door, refusing to move. Even the offer of food will not make him look at her or move. Previously, she had a cat who used to react in the same way to the same place.

And one night, at about 3 a.m., the landlady was woken up by a DVD of Elvis playing really loudly, even though she had carefully turned off the television as usual before going to bed. It still turns on and off by itself but, since the first time, without Elvis's help.

Every Sunday night, the large room on the second floor of the Bear and Billet is filled with the sound of superb music from local and visiting folk musicians, led by Full House, the resident band of the Raven Folk Club. I have never seen the ghost of the young girl, but as I go up the stairs to the Raven, I can usually feel exactly where she is standing. In August 2018, however, I felt nothing. Was she having a night off? I soon found out where she had moved to. During the evening I had a seat next to a table on my right, where I put my drink. In the middle of one act, I heard a noise, looked down, and saw my glass in pieces on the wet carpeted floor. When the lady sitting in front of me complained I had spilled my drink on her, a friend sitting opposite was able to say that nobody had been anywhere near my glass; it had been safely in the middle of the table. When I took the broken glass down to the bar with an apology, the bar staff just told me not to worry, it had been happening a lot recently.

In the space of five weeks, glasses placed safely on tables landed on the floor a total of three times. This could be blamed on the uneven floors but the tables in that room are very big and sturdy. A lady who was on one of my tours some time later told me of a similar experience when she was having a drink on the ground floor.

Then, in 2019, there was a spate of incidents at the Raven Folk Club when guitars leaning securely against a wall were knocked over.

A woman in old-fashioned clothes has been seen on two separate occasions by different people in the ladies' toilets. One lady described the woman as wearing a Victorian dress and pinafore, like a maid. The other lady saw a woman in what she thought was fancy dress. She never heard the woman leave and her husband waiting in the corridor outside saw no one, but when the lady left her cubicle, there was no one there. Could this be the ghost of the servant who died in the upstairs room?

But to return to Ed and the onion. Once the landlady had uttered the cry described at the beginning of this section, she went to fetch Ed, the chef. Ed has seen ghosts since he was a child and, to my surprise, believes there are three at the Bear and Billet.

In December 2019 he opened the pub at about 11 a.m. and went upstairs to the kitchen on the second floor. He was alone: the landlady was still upstairs and the assistant chef had not yet arrived. The vegetable delivery had not yet arrived but he had two red onions so, while he was waiting, he topped and tailed them and walked a couple of steps to put the peelings in the bin, leaving the onions standing on the worktop. When he came back, one of the onions had disappeared. He searched the whole kitchen but could not find it. When the assistant chef arrived and heard the story of the Missing Onion, he looked everywhere too, but with no luck. Throughout the day, every member of staff heard the story, searched but saw not a sign of it. At the end of the day, Ed tidied and cleaned the kitchen, leaving everywhere spotlessly clear and clean, as usual.

The next day, Ed opened the pub, again alone, and went upstairs to the kitchen. And swore. There on the worktop was the red onion.

Ed thinks the ghost of the little boy who haunts the pub had taken the onion, thinking it was a red ball. On a previous occasion, again alone in the kitchen, he had felt someone trying to pick his back pocket: he thinks that, too, was the ghost of the little boy.

One day Ed and the kitchen assistant received a delivery via the goods lift next to the window. The assistant took a 5-litre bottle from the lift and carried it to Ed's bench. As she did so, they both saw mist on the floor near the lift, like a small cloud. It moved like a snake along the floor, under the table, and then disappeared. Ed is adamant it could not have been a reflection, given the way it moved. And as they both saw it, he could not have imagined the cloud.

In September 2020, Ed was getting changed in the staff changing room next to the kitchen when he heard a woman shouting, 'Where's Eddy?' He did not recognise the voice, so he came out into the kitchen to find out who it was. But no one had seen or heard anyone.

And as to being in a fright,
Allow me to remark
That Ghosts have just as good a right In every
way, to fear the light,
As Men to fear the dark.

Lewis Carroll,
Phantasmagoria

Chester Castle Area

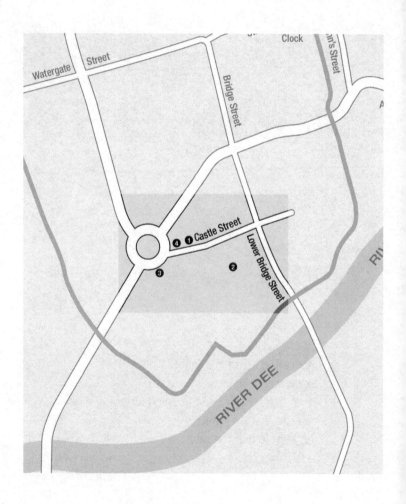

This area encompasses Chester Castle, the Crown Court and Grosvenor Roundabout.

The castle was built by William I in 1070, when it held a prominent position overlooking the city, the harbour and the wide estuary. For centuries it was the seat of power in the area: Edward I and his army headed from here to fight the Welsh; the captive Richard II spent a night here; Jacobites were imprisoned, tried and sentenced to transportation from here.

By the eighteenth century, though, it was deemed unfit for purpose and the surviving medieval and Norman buildings were replaced over forty years from the late 1780s by Thomas Harrison. He created an architectural masterpiece. The complex now houses the Crown Court; part of the University of Chester; a military museum; and the Agricola Tower, which is almost all that is left of the original castle. Queen Victoria stands proudly in the car park, facing the propylaeum, the main entrance gateway.

Next to the castle is Grosvenor Roundabout, which takes traffic from the city over the Grosvenor Bridge, also built by Thomas Harrison. The creation of the roundabout in the 1960s necessitated the destruction of the churchyard of St Bridget's, a church that had been pulled down decades earlier. Most of the graves, including that of Thomas Harrison himself, were moved to the new city cemetery in Blacon. But one grave still remains, all alone, in the middle of Grosvenor roundabout: that of Thomas Gould, a nineteenth-century soldier.

1 18 Castle Street

The Golden Eagle on Castle Street has been serving meals
and ale and providing accommodation to soldiers and visitors
to the courts opposite, whenever necessary, since the early
seventeenth century, and was built on the route the Romans
would have marched along from the fortress to the River Dee.
Nonetheless, some time ago the landlord made his views clear:
'There's no such thing as ghosts,' he said. 'I've never seen a
ghost in this building and I've been here years. They don't exist.'
Despite this strong declaration, there are many stories about the
Golden Eagle. It is unsurprising, given its location, that previous
staff and visitors have seen Roman soldiers marching across the
cellar and through the cellar wall.

Footsteps have also been heard in the attic of the living
accommodation, and a previous landlady's dog would sit

facing a corner of her bedroom, barking at whatever he could see there but refusing to go near it. One night, the landlady woke to feel someone pushing her head backwards into the pillow. As the pressure lessened, a figure floated from the bed to the corner that the dog refused to go near.

2 St Mary's Rectory and St Mary's Hill

Opposite the Golden Eagle is a street named St Mary's Hill, which is named after St Mary-on-the-Hill Church, built in 1350 for the use of the soldiers stationed at Chester Castle. It is now occupied by St Mary's Creative Space, a centre for performing arts. The exterior mainly shows nineteenth-century remodelling but the interior boasts a medieval roof, interesting monuments spanning three centuries and the splendid seventeenth-century tomb of Thomas Gamul and his wife. The Gamuls keep poor company, however: the churchyard is full of criminals, plague victims, women condemned as witches, and many of those who died during the Civil War Siege of Chester.

Perhaps it is one of those people who haunts the building opposite the graveyard, which was built as St Michael's Rectory. A room at the top of this building is always icily cold, whatever the temperature in the other rooms or outside, and its door slams when nobody is near it.

St Mary's Rectory is at the top of St Mary's Hill, which used to be the steepest street in the country, perhaps even in the world, until it became pedestrianised and thus lost the official street designation.

Houses were built some years ago at the bottom of the hill, in Shipgate Street, but the new residents complained they were woken by the sound of cows. This can only be explained by the fact that the site was formerly a dairy, with a herd of cows that provided milk for the city. One night the dairyman died in his sleep, but no one discovered his body until they were alerted by the noise of the cows, increasingly desperate to be milked.

3 **Castle Ditch, Grosvenor Roundabout**

Between the Castle car park and the Grosvenor Roundabout pavement is a ditch that used to lie outside of St Bridget's Churchyard. This was where the bodies of three ladies, hanged for witchcraft in 1656, were buried, witches not being allowed to rest in consecrated ground. Their names were Ellen Beech, Anne Osboston (both from Rainow) and Anne Thornton (from Chester). Ellen was said to have caused the death of a neighbour; Anne Osboston was said to have killed four neighbours through witchcraft; Anne Thornton was accused of killing a three-day-old boy. They were all found guilty and hanged and their ghosts serve to remind us of the terrible injustices inflicted on innocent women in those superstitious times.

4 29 Grosvenor Street

This splendid Victorian Gothic building was commissioned by the Trustee Savings Bank in the mid-nineteenth century. Only a clock by Joyce of Whitchurch would do for a bank as solid as the Trustee. The clock on the tower remains, but the bank moved out some decades ago. Latterly, the building has been used as a restaurant.

I was once enjoying a cup of tea in what is now Suzy K @ The Secret Garden, when the then owner, Sally, told me the story of her breathing problems when she was near the ghost of the monk. I turned to the young lady who was sitting in that same spot, the front window corner, and asked her if she felt anything. She did not, but was eager to tell me her own story of where she worked as a waitress: the restaurant at 29 Grosvenor Street.

The young lady recounted how, before customers arrived at the restaurant in the evenings, a man in a striped shirt would

sometimes enter the restaurant, walk across the floor, and disappear into the kitchens. The person on reception would call him to come back, and when he did not, they would chase after him. But, of course, he had disappeared. And when they returned to the front desk, they would find the door to the street still locked.

When I went to the restaurant later, the manager confirmed the story and also called two members of staff, a waiter and a chef, to tell me their tale. One night, at about midnight, when the two men had been left alone to close up the restaurant, they heard loud, insistent knocking on the door in the cellar leading to the vaults. That door had not been opened for years and they had no way of opening it.

Upstairs on the first floor, wine bottles would move around noisily when the restaurant was empty. The staff had no idea who the ghosts were but, equally, were not happy about sharing the restaurant with them.

What beckoning ghost, along the moonlight shade
invites my steps, and points to yonder glade?

Alexander Pope,
Elegy to the Memory of an Unfortunate Lady

Railway Station Area

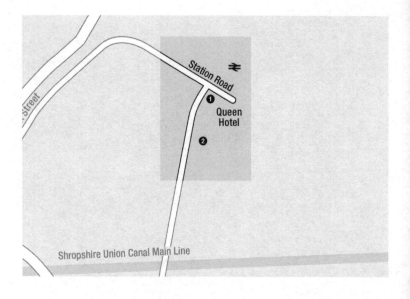

The railways came to Chester three years after Victoria became Queen, hence all the buildings in this area were developed to meet the needs of the railways and their passengers and are thus, however grand or modest, firmly Victorian in style.

Within the space of a few years, Chester had become an important centre of the railway network in the north-west, so its new status demanded a suitably prestigious railway station. The station therefore became the proud owner in 1848 of a facade in a very impressive Italianate style. It was also the longest in the world, stretching almost a quarter of a mile, 350m, from one end to the other.

Before you leave the station, take a moment to find and admire the plaque erected near the entrance in memory of Thomas Brassey, a much-overlooked local man. He was the building contractor for Chester Railway Station but he was also, as the plaque says, 'The World's Foremost Builder of Railways in the 19th Century'. He not only laid 5 per cent of the world's railways before his death, he also found time to build all the necessary bits that went with them, including tunnels, viaducts, docks and stations. Yet, sadly, very few people have heard of him.

The new railways caused a boom in tourism in Chester in the second half of the nineteenth century. Tourists needed hotels, and hotels needed road access to the station, so in 1860 City Road was built. The clock in the centre of the station facade was even moved from the centre to face City Road, so passengers travelling to the station could see whether or not they needed to start running.

1 Queen Hotel

The Queen Hotel opened soon after the building of City Road and became the world's first-ever purpose-built grand railway hotel. It was for first class passengers only, of course. Porters would help them off the train, take care of their luggage, and lead them into the hotel and up to their rooms. The guests did not even have to mix with the hoi polloi on their way to and from the station: the hotel

provided a separate covered walkway under the archway to the left of the main entrance. The Queen Hotel is still a very elegant hotel, both inside and out. But it is a mystery to me why anyone dares stay there, given the number of ghost stories attached to it, most of them very sad.

The walkway area is little used now, apart from by ghosts. At 6.15p.m., on 24 May 1847, passengers boarded a train from Chester to Ruabon. As it crossed the bridge over the River Dee near Chester Racecourse, one of the girders of the bridge, which had been built by Stephenson only five months earlier, broke and all the carriages fell into the river 11 metres below. Five people died and nine were injured. It is said that ghosts often return to the last place on earth where they were happy, hence the reason that those five have sought refuge in the area where the walkway of the Queen Hotel was later built.

A year after it opened, the Queen Hotel was badly damaged by fire and needed extensive rebuilding. The female servants' accommodation on the third floor only suffered smoke damage, though, so just needed repairs. And it was during these repairs that workmen found the mummified remains of a baby under the floorboards of one of the bedrooms. Apparently, one of the servants had given birth in secret in her room and, fearing the severe consequences at that time of having an illegitimate baby, had smothered it and hidden the body. Three months later, full of remorse, she threw herself out of a hotel window and killed herself. Her bedroom is now Room 301, one of five rooms on that floor. Guests who stay on that corridor frequently ring the reception desk to report the screams of a baby.

Down in the cellar, a chef once hanged himself. It is not his ghost who haunts the cellar, though, but that of the traumatised man who found him. Strangely, there are often reports of wet footprints running along the cellar corridor.

In what is now a store-room on the second floor, a woman was chloroformed to death by her male companion. And a skeleton bride is sometimes seen in the background at functions.

However, the most disturbing events happened just before the publication of the first edition of this book. A couple were staying in the Queen Catherine Room (Room 230) in the spring of 2015. At 3 a.m., they ran out of the hotel and refused to re-enter. They had woken up to see a man with blond hair and a moustache, wearing a tailcoat, banging on their window – a physical impossibility, as that room is on the second floor. The man climbed into the room and then into their bed, at which point the couple left. A few weeks later, a lady staying in the same room was very distressed to see a man at the end of the bed staring at her and bouncing his hands on the end of the bed. She ran downstairs to report the intruder at reception. Her description confirmed it was the same man.

As far as I know, there has been little ghost activity in the hotel recently.

While first class passengers stayed at the Queen Hotel, second class passengers stayed at the hotel on the opposite corner, which is now the Town Crier.

All other passengers, as well as the hundreds of workers who found employment on the railways, stayed in the streets of proud Victorian terraces that still surround the station.

Hundreds of workers and passengers needed pubs to provide food, drink and entertainment.

2 Bridgewater Arms

The Bridgewater Arms was built on the corner of Crewe Street, a few minutes' walk from the station, and it served refreshments to both travellers and employees. One customer, George, was a regular at the pub for sixty years until his death in 2011. Since then he has been seen in the lounge and 'his' table has been seen wobbling, perhaps as he sits down for a pint and a chat.

Sadly, a barmaid hanged herself in the cellar, and since then an oppressive atmosphere has been felt in it – so much so that a dog owned by a customer on a guided tour recently could not be made to go down the stairs.

Whenever I take up a newspaper, I seem to see ghosts gliding between the lines. There must be ghosts all the country over, as thick as the sand of the sea…

Henrik Ibsen,
Ghosts

Cow Lane Area

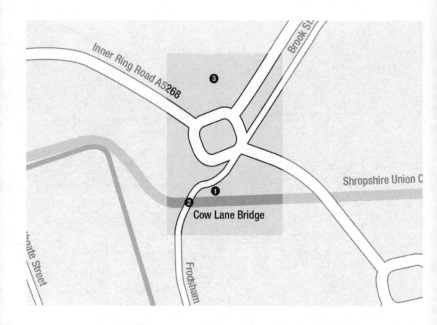

Cow Lane Bridge

Cow Lane Bridge spans the Shropshire Union Canal, and links the station area to the city centre via Brook Lane and Frodsham Street. Through its name it retains the memory of the city's cattle market. Originally the market had been on Northgate Street, hence the names of pubs there that are linked to animals: the Pied Bull, the Bull and Stirrup. As Chester became more genteel, though, the market and its smells were moved to the Cow Lane area, on the site of what is now the bus station. Eventually, the growth of Chester's suburbs on that side of town meant the cattle market had to move right out of town, to Beeston, in 1869.

1 Bingo Hall, Brookdale Place

The Mecca Bingo Hall is on the approach to the bridge. It originally opened as a cinema in 1931, complete with a Mock Tudor frontage and Italianate ceiling mouldings. Nobody can explain the thumping and dragging noises emanating from the upper rooms, noises that were first heard by fire watchers during World War Two and which have been heard from time to time ever since.

2 Canal

Chester's canal system was built during the second half of the eighteenth century and the first half of the nineteenth. The men working on the first section had a much easier time than anticipated, though, when they started to tackle the stretch that passed under the walls on the north side of the city. They were delighted to find the Romans had already done a lot of the work for them: they discovered the deep, overflowing ditch between the city wall and the northern suburbs was actually a cutting made by the Romans over 1,500 years previously.

By the mid-nineteenth century, Chester had become a major canal port in the north-west. This was just as well, as Liverpool by then had completely dwarfed Chester in its amount of river and sea shipping.

As you cross over Cow Lane Bridge on your way into town, pause for a moment and look into the waters of the canal below.

Sometimes a mist can be seen over the water and a pale grey figure rises out of it. Sometimes a Viking runs along the bank in horror, pain and fear, having been flayed alive by some of the good people of Chester.

3 St Anne Street

The suburb of Newtown, a maze of terraced houses, is visible from Cow Lane Bridge. This area was built mainly for railway workers, and the street at right angles to St Anne Street is called Black Diamond Street, black diamond being another word for the coal that was transported to, from and through Chester by train.

In the latter half of the nineteenth century, a family moved into one of the houses in St Anne's Street. It was immediately disturbed every night by the sound of footsteps going up the stairs and stopping at the children's bedroom door. One night, the bravest of the children got out of bed and opened the door; there was nobody there. After that, the family took to pulling the blankets over their heads and trying to ignore the footsteps. Some time later, the fam-

ily heard loud noises from the living room fireplace, and came downstairs to find several books had fallen down the chimney into the fire, burning before the family could retrieve them. From that moment onwards, the nightly footsteps stopped.

Where'er we tread, 't is haunted, holy ground.

Lord Byron,
Childe Harold's Pilgrimage

Amphitheatre &
River Dee Area

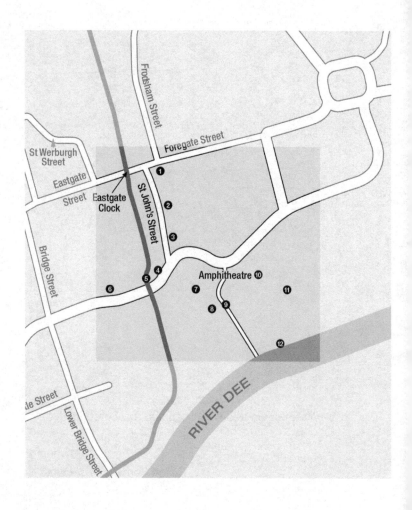

This walk takes you down St John Street, along Pepper and Little St John Streets, into the amphitheatre, round St John's Church, and finally down to the River Dee. You will read a lot of strange stories on the way. And might even see some strange things yourself.

1 Blossoms Hotel, St John Street

The Blossoms Hotel's full name is actually The New Blossoms Hotel, because it is the third of that name to occupy the corner of St John's Street and Foregate Street. The present one was built in 1650, though, so it can, and does, lay claim to be the oldest hotel in Chester. So it is unsurprising that there are at least two ghosts here.

Room 206 in the Blossoms Hotel is haunted, according to staff; a bedside lamp has been seen flickering on and off even when the lamp is not switched on.

Many years ago a porter saw a man in the middle of the night on the first floor. The man, wearing seventeenth-century clothes, asked the time of the next coach to York. And then promptly turned round and walked through a wall.

2 3 St John Street

The Marlbororough Arms is a Victorian rebuild, but it has kept its original frontage. And, yes, the spelling is correct and the extra two letters in the name of the Marlbororough Arms are due, of course, to a ghost in the cellar. (Did you notice the unusual spelling before I pointed it out?) The ghost was a landlord of the pub who killed himself by cutting his throat in the cellar, and he can be still heard bemoaning his fate. Years after his death, another (living) landlord asked a painter to paint a new sign above the front window. The painter had only completed half of the name when he was struck with a dreadful thirst. There was only one thing to do: he went down into the cellar and poured himself a tankard of beer, which he was quietly enjoying when he became aware of the moans, groans and gurglings of the dead landlord's ghost and his cut throat. The painter shot up the stairs, ran up the ladder, hastily finished the pub sign, slid down the ladder and ran off, never to be seen again. It was only later that the landlord noticed the spelling mistake.

In the 1980s there was an all-night vigil with paranormal investigators at the pub. Nothing was seen, but photos were taken which clearly showed a large white orb hovering above a table. On another occasion a large barrel in the cellar was pushed towards a psychic researcher.

In the 1970s the landlord and landlady used an intercom to monitor their baby asleep in the pram. The device, though, would often pick up voices in an otherwise empty room. Later, the little boy would ride up and down the long corridor in the staff quarters on his trike, only getting off when a man appeared, blocking his way. The parents could never see the man – he was only visible to the child.

There is also the story of a lady in grey who stands by the bar, ready to serve customers. One member of staff dismissed all the ghost stories, but a young man on one of my ghost tours in the winter of 2014 told me he had seen the lady at the bar when he was drinking there the previous weekend, and was baffled when nobody else could see her.

3 **2 St John's Street**

Above what is currently Zuger's Tea Rooms is what used to be Chester's telephone exchange. In October 2017, as my ghost tour group and I passed by en route for the amphitheatre, a Chester resident who was on the tour stopped and pointed to a window on the top floor. She was once employed by the telephone exchange based in the building, and said she had once been working alone in that room when she heard a man walking up and down in the corridor outside. She was so

scared she rang the engineer in another part of the building to ask him to come and see who the man was and how he had got into the building, as it was closed to the public. When the engineer came, he did a thorough search but there was no sign of anyone apart from them in the building. I have heard from another resident of Chester who worked in the same building that the caretaker would get very annoyed with whoever was in the empty building, because he, she or it kept flinging the chairs across one of the rooms during the night.

4 South East Angle Tower

All four Angle Towers of the Roman fortress were guarded day and night by soldiers. One night, the captain of the guard at the South East Angle Tower was tempted away into the fields by a beautiful Welsh girl. When he returned, all his men had been murdered. It was obvious they had been killed by Welsh men, but we can only speculate as to whether it was in revenge for a dishonoured daughter, or whether she was really a wicked

Welsh woman who deliberately lured the captain away with her womanly wiles while others came in and committed their dastardly deeds. Whatever the truth, there was only one course of action open

to the captain: he buried the hilt of his sword in the ground and fell on it. His ghost now wanders that part of the walls, a fact confirmed a few years ago by a student of the University of Chester. She was taking her usual early morning run around the walls and saw him clearly on the Newgate Bridge as she approached it. As she got nearer, though, he became fainter, and he had disappeared completely when she reached the spot where he had been.

5 Newgate Bridge

Until 1938, the only way into Chester when passing the amphitheatre was through the Wolfgate, which you can see to one side of the Newgate. Now, only pedestrians can walk through the Wolfgate, but until the Newgate Bridge was opened there was severe traffic congestion along this stretch of Pepper Street. It is sobering to think that all the other main gates to Chester, controlling traffic in and out of the city, were a similar size until they were replaced.

The Newgate Bridge has towers on either side of it with rooms that are sometimes open during the day in the tourist

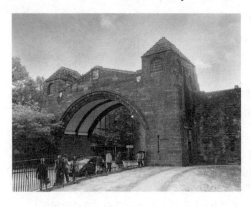

season. After I had finished telling the previous story of the captain of the guard during a ghost tour in the winter of 2015, however, one member of the group asked me who the man in the right-hand tower was. 'There is nobody up there,' I said. 'Yes there is,' she said, 'I have been watching him all the time you were telling that last story.' I was adamant that the city council would never pay for anyone to man the tower room late at night at Hallowe'en, even if it was near the ruins of the South East Angle Tower; she was equally adamant that she had seen a man walking backwards and forwards in the room all the time we had been standing there.

6 The Methodist Chapel, Pepper Street

For many years, all knowledge and sight of the chapel, now clearly visible with its wonderful frontage, were hidden under the facade of a service station and car showroom on this site. It was revealed in all its glory, however, when it became the centrepiece of a new dining area in Chester in 2015. The service station had gradually lost customers as supermarkets started selling petrol at much lower prices. In an effort to stave off defeat, the owner had opened the service station longer

and longer in the evenings, but found it hard to keep male staff because of the ghosts. While the employee filled a car with petrol, two monks would often appear from the shadows and stand silently watching what he was doing, then slip back into the shadows when he had finished. No man could stand that for long. But one young lady found she had no problem with the ghosts, even naming them Charlie and Herbert and trying to engage them in conversation. The monks remained silent, however, slipping in and out of the shadows. When the premises became a furniture store, first Habitat and then Le Chateau, the monks were never seen again.

However, since the Methodist Chapel has become a restaurant, someone has been joining the diners. One Saturday night, my group and I approached the chapel, and as there was a bouncer on duty, I asked if he minded if we stopped while I told my story. 'Not a problem,' he said. 'You can come and listen if you want to,' I replied. But he just looked down at his shoes and muttered no. 'Why not?' 'I've already seen him.' 'Who?' Along with the beautiful entrance, the renovations had also uncovered two elegant staircases on either side. The bouncer, it appeared, had frequently seen a man in black going up the stairs on the right, even though he knew full well that the doors top and bottom were both locked.

This ghost's presence was confirmed in November 2017, when I stopped my ghost tour party on the other side of the road, facing the Methodist Chapel. Before I had begun to tell my story, a lady in the group shouted out that she could see him – a man in a long black coat in front of the right-hand staircase.

7 The Old Convent/Amphitheatre

Chester's amphitheatre is the biggest in Britain. The first amphitheatre, built *c*. AD 70, was wooden, but in the year 100

it was replaced by a magnificent stone amphitheatre with a diameter of 315ft (96m), curved walls 8½ft (2.5m) thick and a height of 40ft (12m). It could seat 7,000 people, more than there were soldiers in the fortress, so it was obviously used to entertain the local civilian population, too, as well as show off the might of the Roman army. It was abandoned along with the fortress at the end of the fourth century, and then, somehow, it was hidden for over 1,500 years.

It was only discovered in 1929 when a workman, digging in what was then the grounds of Dee House, an Ursuline Convent, found a coin that turned out to have the head of Hadrian stamped on it. The workman's next discovery was a curved stone wall. He had found the long-lost amphitheatre of the Fortress Deva.

A few years later, this unique find did not make the good leaders of Chester change their plans for the road improvements through the new bridge; they could not see any reason why they should not build a straight road from the Newgate to St John's Church, straightening the existing loop and going right over the amphitheatre. Fortunately, the Chester Archaeological Society led a long, hard and successful campaign and the existing loop remained, as did the amphitheatre.

Gladiators fought in Chester's Roman Amphitheatre on more than 200 days of every year during their stay in Fortress Deva, apart from when they popped up north to build a huge section of Hadrian's Wall. I would therefore expect it to be teeming with the ghosts of fallen gladiators or soldiers, even those of criminals who had been executed there. However, in the first edition of this book, I wrote that there was not a single ghost in the amphitheatre. In my research when I first became a ghost tour guide, I had found not a single story, and I had heard not a single tale in all the years since. Indeed, this lack of ghosts had been confirmed by a man on one of my ghost tours who could see ghosts and had seen a ghost waiting at each of the stops I had made with the group. You cannot get better verification than that! However, in September 2019, a young lady on one of my ghost tours told of going to the amphitheatre twenty-four years previously, on a day trip with her grandparents when she was only 2 years old. She still remembered very clearly asking her grandparents why there were soldiers in the amphitheatre. The grandparents, of course, could not see them, but she could see a group of them standing together on the floor of the amphitheatre. She was particularly interested as none of them had any feet.

The other ghost in the area is a lady in white who carries a lamp and walks to and fro on the top floor of Dee House, the Georgian/Victorian house built over part of the amphitheatre. Nobody knows who the ghost is, perhaps someone from the family who lived there originally, or perhaps one of the nuns who lived there when it was a convent, or even the ghost of a pupil from the convent school who has been kept in detention a bit too long. At the moment the building is unoccupied, but workers did report feeling someone was watching them when they were in an upstairs room while closing up the building. Other workmen who went into the cellar to turn off the electricity were somewhat scared to see poltergeist activity while they were down there.

The lady's lamplight is sometimes seen on dark nights. In fact, at the beginning of September 2017, a couple returned to Dee House for a further look after finishing one of my ghost tours. They had been intrigued by the story of the lady's lamplight, but as it was still too light when my group were there, they waited until dark and returned. They were rewarded with a very clear photo of a light shining in a first-floor window. Some people who have looked closely at it are sure they can see a lady standing in the window, in front of the light. Since then, there have been a few more sightings of the light, the latest being in the winter of 2019.

8 Old Bishop's Palace

The Old Bishop's Palace is behind the amphitheatre, overlooking the River Dee. Now used as a wedding venue, it was built in the mid-eighteenth century and was the residence of the Bishops of Chester until the 1920s. It was also where a shoe shine boy lived until he was thrown out by a jealous housekeeper. He may have died of starvation, but his ghost still returns to hide shoes and move them around.

9 Anchorite Cell

The Anchorite Cell is a sandstone building on a sandstone outcrop behind St John's Church, overlooking the River Dee. It is now a private residence but was built originally as a hermitage. The present building dates from the mid-fourteenth

century. There have been many reports of poltergeist activity in the building, but in 2005, when the poltergeist threw all the crockery off the owner's dresser, the owner had had enough and wrote to her insurance company for compensation. Amazingly, she won.

Chester's most mysterious ghost is a monk who walks along the path by the old bell tower on the west side of St John's Church. He first started appearing after the bell tower collapsed in the middle of the night on Good Friday 1881. Most unusually for a ghost, the monk is desperate to talk to the people he meets. In 2011 a young couple saw him walking towards them, but they ran away when they realised they could only see the upper part of his body. Other people who have heard him talk, however, cannot understand what he says because, it appears, he is talking in old Anglo-Saxon English and what he is trying to tell them is his identity: King Harold Godwinson, who was defeated at the Battle of

Hastings in 1066. According to the Bayeux Tapestry, Harold died on the battlefield after being killed by an arrow in his eye, but history is always embroidered by the victors.

The truth, as Harold is so keen to tell people, is that he was only blinded in one eye. He escaped to Europe and later came in disguise to Chester for one good reason: his wife, Queen Ealdgyth, had been placed in the convent at Chester. From the moment he took up residence in the Anchorite Cell, she visited every day, bringing him wine, bread and meat until the day he died. Many years ago, excavations in the grounds of the Anchorite Cell found two skeletons: those of a male and a female, lying side by side.

This story is verified by none other than Giraldus Cambrensis, Gerald of Wales, who wrote an account of his travels round Wales in 1188. His *Itinerarium Cambriae*, or *The Journey Through Wales*, published in 1191, describes how he spent three nights in Chester over the Easter weekend. He wrote: 'Having received many wounds, and lost his left eye by an arrow ... he is said to have escaped to these parts [Chester], where, in holy conversation, leading the life of an anchorite, and being a constant attendant at one of the churches of this city, he is believed to have terminated his days happily.' Perhaps it is time to rewrite the history books.

10 St John the Baptist's Church

St John the Baptist's Church is next to the Roman amphitheatre; indeed, many of its foundations are recycled amphitheatre stones. According to legend, Ethelred, the King of Mercia, built St John's Church in 689, although Revd

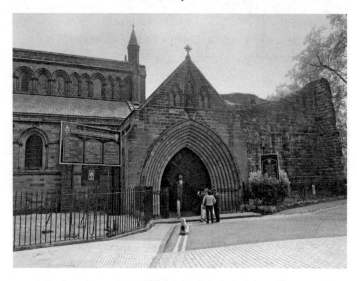

Chesters, the current vicar of St John's, believes it may date from much earlier. It is certainly Chester's oldest church and was, for many years, its most important. In 973, King Edgar insisted nine princes rowed him upriver to St John's from near the village of Handbridge, in order to show their submission to his authority.

In the tenth and eleventh centuries, it was a very important centre for the established Church and had a large parish. It was even a cathedral from 1075 to 1085. The Normans gave it a splendid, still existing, nave and crossing in the twelfth century, and it remained an ecclesiastical hub until the late fifteenth century, when it was reduced to simply a parish church. As a result, the thirteenth- and fourteenth-century chapels to the east of the church were allowed to fall into the picturesque but moody ruins we see today. The collapse of the bell tower at the west side of the church in

1881 only added to its atmosphere. It is by the ruins of this tower that the ghost of Harold is sometimes seen.

But ghosts also walk elsewhere in the ruins of St John's. In the ruins at the east end of the church there is a coffin set into the wall. The coffin is made from a tree trunk and the inside is inscribed with words from the Church of England burial service: *Dust to Dust*. Nobody knows for sure how it came to be there, but it is linked to the ghost of a lady in white who wanders the ruins underneath. Perhaps it is the ghost of a nun who asked for her coffin to be placed as near to God as possible. Or is it the ghost of a young lady who married an old gentleman? He became so jealously possessive after the wedding that she was allowed to receive no visitors or to leave the house. When she eventually died, her husband had her coffin placed high on the wall so that nobody could walk over her grave; perhaps she wanders round the ruins looking for it to this day.

During Hallowe'en 2015, all the ghost guides of Chester were out in force conducting ghost tours around the city until late in the evening. At about ten o' clock, when one group was leaving St John's ruins, one lady and her friend decided to leave the tour group as she was tired. While the group disappeared

down the steps towards the river, the lady decided to take photographs of Grosvenor Park opposite the ruins, which looked, she explained later, so peaceful and quiet. I was shown the photos the next day because the lady had been so astonished at what she noticed in them, she had taken them to the Visitor Information Centre: on the left of the photo, she believed, there was a heavily bearded man holding a baby; on the right was a monk with his arms folded across his chest as though he had just left his coffin.

I was not surprised when I saw the photograph; I had already heard the story of local photographer David Mitchell, who had taken the photos that featured on the covers of the first edition of this book. When he printed the photos he had taken that night, he was shocked to discover the outline of someone dressed in red on some of the photos. We had been completely alone in the ruins that evening.

Again, a tourist popped into St John's church one day to have a welcome cup of tea and flick through all the photos he had taken both inside and around the outside of the church. The volunteer heard his shocked cry when he saw a monk in some of the photos, standing in the ruins.

In July 2018, a dental nurse I know said that she, her friend and their boyfriends were walking past St John's Church on the footpath, heading in the direction of Grosvenor Park. It was about two o'clock in the morning but the ladies had not been drinking because they were the designated drivers. The four were walking in pairs on the narrow footpath, the ladies behind the men, when they heard a woman suddenly talking very loudly close behind them. The two ladies turned round and saw someone dressed as a nun. The fact that the nun had seemingly come from nowhere was a shock in itself, but when they realised the nun had no feet, just legs that did not touch the floor, they both turned and screamed at their boyfriends. But when all four turned around again, the nun had gone.

Is this the same nun that someone on one of my tours photographed on the pavement between Grosvenor Park and the ruins of St John's? Her photograph clearly shows a figure in a long, black outfit. Is she perhaps the nun whose coffin is possibly the one on the wall of St John's ruins?

11 Grosvenor Park

In the 1860s, the 2nd Marquess of Westminster, Richard, bought 20 acres of land in Chester, overlooking the river. He pulled down the houses that were there, turned the area into a beautiful park with the help of the renowned landscape architect Edward Kemp, and gave it to the local council, who promptly employed a man called Billy Hobby to open and shut all the gates each morning and night. Billy loved his job so much that he is still doing it to this day, much to the annoyance of people who cross the park to get to work. One of my colleagues at the college in Handbridge, where I worked some years ago, often complained to the council that she had to take a long diversion because the gates were locked. The council was always adamant they had indeed been unlocked on those mornings.

One night, a tour group was standing by the gates to the park near St John's Church, listening to the guide tell the tale of Billy, when they clearly heard the chains on the gates rattling.

12 The River Dee

The River Dee is one of the reasons why the Romans built a fortress here. With a strong tide and an estuary 2 miles wide at the time, it was perfect for bringing ships right into the harbour by what is now Chester's racecourse. The river has become more and more narrow over the centuries as it flows from Lake Bala in Wales down to the Irish Sea, but it is still very popular with Cestrians and tourists alike.

However, 1801 marked a sad but notable day in its history: in that year, a man called John Clare and two other unfortunate men were taken from the Northgate Gaol to Gallows Hill in Boughton by cart to be executed. Executions were great public spectacles at the time, so the crowd milling round the cart was huge and boisterous. John Clare managed to escape and ran down the hill to the river, sure that nobody could capture him but forgetting the weight of his chains. He drowned and his body was recovered by the hangman, only to be taken back to Gallows Hill to be hanged in front of a now shocked crowd and the two other terrified men. The hangman was paid by the hanging, not the dead body, and he wanted to ensure full payment. That was the last public hanging in Chester, but John Clare still reminds us of the sorry tale as he wanders the banks of the River Dee.

Look out, too, for the ghost of a lady wearing a long black gown and black headdress, believed to be that of a nun who drowned in the river.

13 Old Dee Bridge

The Old Dee Bridge is on the site of the first bridge over the River Dee in this area; in fact, the only one over the Dee in Chester until the nineteenth century. The first to be built here was a stone bridge erected by the Romans. This was followed by a number of unsuccessful wooden medieval bridges, and even a ferry, until the solid structure that exists today was erected in 1387. It had a fortified gatepost on the far side until the 1780s, tolls until 1885, and at one point, after the bridge had been widened, there was a huge five-storey mill looming over the Bridgegate area.

A man was walking home from work across the Old Dee Bridge one day in the 1960s, when he stopped to chat to a neighbour who was walking into town. They had a lovely little chat, caught up on a few bits of gossip, and then both went on their way. When he got home, his wife told him the neighbour had died that morning.

Sometimes, when people stop on the bridge to admire the views, they can smell burning and hear shrieks; these are the ghostly echoes of a fire in the mill on the Dee Bridge in the late nineteenth century, in which two people died.

And so ends the journey round the haunted buildings of Chester – a journey that will never be complete. Some ghosts may fade away and never be seen again, but there will always be others waiting to take their places. The story of Chester's ghosts is never-ending, and Chester can truly lay claim to be the most actively haunted town in the country.

The ghost of Caesar hath appeared to me two, several times by night; at Sardis once; and, this last night, here in Philippi fields. I know my hour is come.

William Shakespeare,
Julius Caesar

Postscript

On 28 March 2015, two men joined my ghost tour and heard the story at the start of this book – that of the head in the flat in the converted old house in a suburb of Chester. 'I bet that's the house we lived in,' said one.

After the tour, I confirmed that it was indeed the same one. They had lived in Flat 1 on the ground floor of the house for twenty years, until September 2014, and had experienced constant ghost activity during that time.

During the day they would regularly see someone walk past the lounge window, but whenever they looked out of the window, there was nobody there. They often heard people walking around the flat.

In the early hours of one morning, one of them was making a sandwich in the kitchen when he heard women talking in the lounge. The chatter stopped when he went into the lounge – as soon, it seemed, as the women noticed him. There was nobody in the room.

One Sunday night, at 10.15 p.m., they were both watching television when they saw a blue, pulsating orb rising up in front of the closed door. Two weeks later, on a Saturday afternoon, they saw a blue light about the size of a golf ball in the same area; it went through the open door and moved towards the bedroom.

They often heard children running up and down the stairs in the early hours of the morning and could never understand why nobody from the other flats in the building mentioned them. The only time they heard the children during the day was when one of the men decided to demolish a cupboard under the stairs, by the simple but effective method of hitting it with a very large hammer. As soon as he made the first hole, he heard the sound of the children's footsteps running from the cupboard and up the stairs. Once he had finished his demolition job, the children were never heard again.

The men never once felt frightened or threatened.

Bibliography

Ackroyd, P., 'The English Ghost', *The Telegraph*, 29 October 2011

Armand, M., *The Ghosts of Cheshire* (Wirral: Birkenhead Press Limited, 1989)

Brandon, D., *Haunted Chester* (Stroud: The History Press Ltd, 2008)

Carrington, P., *Chester* (London: B.T. Batsford Ltd, 1994)

Hall, S., 'Sarah, the Spook in the Sweet Shop', *The Chronicle*, 21 October 2005, p.32

Langtree, S. and Comyns, A., *200 Years of Building* (Chester: The Chester Civic Trust, 2001)

Matthews, R., *Haunted Chester* (Eastleigh: Pitkin Pictorials Limited, 2008)

Slemen, T., *Haunted Cheshire* (Liverpool: Bluecoat Press, 2011)

Stephens, R., *Chester* (Barnsley: Pen and Sword Books Ltd, 2006)

Ward, S., *Chester: A History* (Chichester: Phillimore & Co. Ltd, 2009)

Wilding, R., *Death in Chester* (Bath: Gordon Emery, 2003)

Wolfe, J., *Aethelflaed Royal Lady, War Lady* (Chester: Fenris Press, 2001)

Acknowledgements

Grateful thanks to the following people for giving their time and skills so freely:

Maria Barnard, Senior Sales Advisor, Browns of Chester, 2001–21;

Revd Chesters, Rector of St John's Church;

Rodger Martin, graphic designer;

Members of the Guild of Chester Tour Guides who contributed their tales: Ann Coward, Mike Hewitt, Virginia Jordan, Alan Mealing, Martin Nield, Christine Philips, Liz Roberts, Roger Stephens, Jean Sullivan, Jan Varley;

The shops, restaurants and hotels of Chester, especially the managers of the Bear and Billet, Bollicini, the Boot Inn, El Gato Negro, The Scented Garden, Suzie K @ the Secret Garden, Queen Hotel;

The residents of Chester who have provided many of the stories in this book, some still with us only in spirit …

There are more things in heaven and earth, Horatio,
than are dreamed of in your philosophy.

William Shakespeare,
Hamlet